RAND

Substance Abuse Problems and Programs in Newark

A Needs Assessment for Newark's Fighting Back Initiative

Patricia A. Ebener, Peter W. Greenwood
with Jeffrey Fagan

Supported by the
Boys' and Girls' Clubs of Newark

Drug Policy Research Center

Preface

This report describes the nature and extent of substance abuse problems in Newark, their effects on the community, and the programs and resources currently addressing them. Because it focuses primarily on the city's problems, this report does not present a very flattering portrait. Indeed, some of the figures it contains are quite depressing. However, Newark is not alone in possessing these problems. Any city of significant size will have its own pockets of high-risk residents exhibiting many of the same problems of self-destructive behavior. What does set Newark apart is its determination to recognize these problems, and mobilize the resources to bring about change. The study was commissioned by the Boys' and Girls' Clubs of Newark, the lead agency in the Newark Fighting Back Initiative. The objective of this initiative is to develop intensive, community-wide activities that will help reduce local drug use and its attendant problems.

Additional support for this study came from RAND's Drug Policy Research Center, with funding from the Ford and Weingart foundations. This work is part of the center's extensive and ongoing assessment of drug problems and policies at local and national levels. The study should be of interest to Newark's community leaders and to the agencies and organizations involved in the Newark Fighting Back Initiative. It should also be of interest to policy researchers attempting to interpret existing drug abuse indicators in other communities.

v

Contents

Figures

Tables

Summary

Overview

Newark is the largest city in New Jersey, with a 1990 population of 275,221 residents who, compared to other cities, are disproportionately poor, black, and residing in single-parent, female-headed households. It is also one of the nation's fastest-shrinking cities, having lost 16 percent of its population during the past decade.

The city's drug and alcohol culture is well entrenched and affects a large fraction of the population. Newark has one of the highest rates of crime and AIDS of any American city, with particularly high rates of homicide, robbery, and auto theft. Fifty to sixty percent of its chronic, long-term intravenous drug–user population is HIV positive. As of April 1991, the city had documented 2,233 cases of AIDS. Excluding pediatric cases, 69 percent of the AIDS cases involved intravenous drug users.

In 1989, The Boys' and Girls' Clubs of Newark, along with similar agencies in 14 other cities, was awarded a 2-year planning grant under the auspices of the Robert Wood Johnson Foundation's Fighting Back Program. The purpose of the grant was to develop a comprehensive community plan designed to reduce demand for illegal drugs. One of the foundation's requirements for subsequent funding was clear documentation of the city's current drug problems and efforts to deal with them.

In December of 1990, The Boys' and Girls' Clubs of Newark commissioned RAND to perform a needs assessment to support their Fighting Back planning effort. This report presents the findings of that study. It includes an analysis of various measures that reflect the nature and extent of drug problems in Newark and their impact on the community. It also contains information on the nature of drug markets and drug dealing in Newark, obtained from interviews with drug dealers, and from analyses of police and court data regarding the characteristics and disposition of a sample of adults arrested for selling drugs in Newark. The report also describes the number, characteristics, and utilization of programs available in 1991–1992 within the city for the treatment and/or prevention of drug use and concludes with a number of recommendations for dealing with substance abuse problems in Newark.

Most of the Newark Fighting Back (NFB) project's efforts during the planning period were directed toward the problems of citizens residing within a neighborhood comprising approximately 72 square blocks centered on the intersection of Spruce Street and Martin Luther King Boulevard in the city's Central Ward. This target neighborhood exhibits all of the city's substance abuse problems in their most acute forms. Previous census data have shown that 60 percent of the neighborhood's population over 15 years old is female, and many of these women were unemployed. Fifty-four percent of Newark's emergency room episodes relating to cocaine abuse involved residents of the three zip codes that include the target neighborhood, even though the population of this area represents only 26 percent of the city's total. Emergency room patients from this area appear to have severe, chronic problems of heroin abuse.

The general plan of the Fighting Back project is to develop and test programs in this target neighborhood, which can then be adapted and applied to other neighborhoods within the city.

Trends In Substance Abuse Indicators

Drug Abuse Warning Network

The Drug Abuse Warning Network (DAWN) is a federally sponsored database containing information on emergency room episodes related to drug abuse and on drug-related deaths, as reported by county medical examiners. Data for July 1989 to September 1990 show that, on a per capita basis, the number of emergency room episodes associated with cocaine and heroin abuse in Newark consistently exceeded the numbers in Chicago, New York, Los Angeles, and Washington, D.C. During the third quarter of 1989 and the second quarter of 1990, Newark had twice as many heroin-related episodes per hundred thousand population as the next highest metropolitan area.

While the number of emergency room drug episodes within the greater Newark metropolitan region declined substantially between the fourth quarters of 1988 and 1989, as they did in the nation as a whole, the number of drug episodes involving Newark residents increased by 11 percent.

Between January 1987 and December 1989, the drugs contributing to the largest increase in emergency room episodes in Newark were cocaine and heroin, often used in combination. The frequency of episodes involving heroin increased by 50 percent between 1988 and 1989. The number of episodes involving residents from the target neighborhood declined between 1988 and 1989, while the number from the rest of the city increased.

Overall, the DAWN Emergency Room data for 1987 through 1989 show a consistent pattern of an increasing number of drug episodes, heavy involvement of females, and a rapid increase in the number of heroin episodes. These trends are also suggested by arrest data from the Newark Police Department.

Arrests for drug *possession* in the city increased by almost 24 percent between the second half of 1989 and the second half of 1990, a period when enforcement efforts were also increasing. The fraction of cases involving heroin increased from 12.5 to 20.7 percent. Within the target neighborhood, the fraction of cases involving heroin increased by more than 300 percent.

Arrests for drug *sales* within the city held about constant between the two years. However, the percentage of cases involving heroin increased from 15.5 to 25.5 in the city and from 17.8 to 36.4 in the target neighborhood.

Most of the arrestees were males in their twenties. The percentage of females arrested in the sectors that included the target neighborhood was somewhat higher than the rest of the city. This was especially the case for sales: 20 percent of the arrestees in the target area were females, versus 12 percent in the rest of the city. This difference may reflect the greater percentage of females in the population in that part of the city or perhaps special enforcement activity at the time.

Surveys of High School Students

The New Jersey Department of Law and Public Safety has periodically surveyed high school students about their use of drugs. A comparison of responses to the 1980, 1986, and 1989 surveys shows a considerable decline in drug use among this population. New Jersey youth *attending school* are reporting using remarkably fewer drugs, a trend also observed in national surveys.

The survey data show that the lifetime prevalence rate for alcohol as well as for all drugs has steadily declined among the students and that there are no substantial differences by area of the state or by socioeconomic status of the school. The data also showed that, while the perceived availability of marijuana is down, the perceived availability of cocaine and hallucinogens is up.

The Substance Abuse Treatment Population

The New Jersey Department of Health maintains a statewide episode-based data system on drug treatment center admissions. This system contains information on demographic and social characteristics of treatment clientele, their drug-use history, and drug-use characteristics at admission. In November 1990, 55 percent of the clientele in publicly funded substance abuse treatment was admitted for heroin and other opiates, 30 percent for cocaine, 3 percent for alcohol, and 8 percent for other drugs. The December 1990 Community Epidemiology Working Group report for Newark showed that, among the treatment admissions between January and June of 1990, 73 percent had used heroin and 59 percent had used cocaine. Information provided by one of the treatment centers showed that, between 1989 and 1991, the caseload increased by 29 percent from Newark and by 39 percent from the target neighborhood.

Consequences of Drug Abuse Problems for the Community

In a telephone survey conducted in 1989, 68 percent of the people interviewed in Newark agreed that drug dealing was a major problem. In the target neighborhood, a survey of tenants in a Section 8 apartment building in 1991 showed that 88 percent of those surveyed believed that drug abuse was a problem of the highest priority. Unemployment was the only problem given higher priority.

The overall crime rate is also a serious problem. According to the Uniform Crime Reports compiled by the FBI, Newark has one of the highest crime rates per capita in the country, with 14,331 index offenses per 100,000 population reported in 1989, compared to a national average of 5,741. (Index offenses include murder, forcible rape, robbery, aggravated assault, burglary, larceny-theft, and motor vehicle theft.)

The environment of crime, poverty, and drugs has had a strong negative effect on the city's youth. In 1988, 93 percent of the teenagers who gave birth were unwed mothers, accounting for 15 percent of all live births in Newark that year and about 10 percent of the female high-school age population. According to 1980 census data, 25 percent of all births in Newark were to mothers under 20 years old. This is the highest rate of young mothers among the major cities in the country.

In a study of healthy adolescents 12 to 22 years old who were attending an inner city medical clinic in Newark between November 1987 and April 1988, researchers found a total lifetime prevalence rate for major depressive disorders of 30 percent among those surveyed, many of whom reported recurrent episodes. The rate of stressful life events among the population surveyed was quite high, with 17 percent reporting that one or both parents had died, 50 percent reporting xv

that they had witnessed violence, and 8 percent reporting that they had been a victim of sexual abuse.

School dropout rates are another indicator of the pressures and problems facing Newark's youth. The available data do not allow precise estimates of dropout rates; however, after excluding those who transfer among school districts, they do facilitate rough estimates. For example, tracking the dropout rate from Newark high schools for an entering cohort in Fall 1986, and assuming the group remained within the Newark public school system, suggests that as many as 38 percent would have dropped out by June of 1990. Until last year, when a large decrease in dropouts occurred, the dropout rate was even higher at Central High School, which serves the target neighborhood. Compared to other major cities, Newark had the lowest percentage of college graduates among its residents who were 25 years old and over. In 1980, the rate was only 6.3 percent in Newark.

Health indicators also reflect a severe and impoverished environment. Among all the cities in New Jersey, Newark has the highest number of infant, neonatal, and postneonatal deaths; the highest number of low-birthweight babies and births to adolescents; the highest number of adult and pediatric AIDS cases; and the highest number of syphilis, gonorrhea, and clinically active tuberculosis cases.

Premature births (the incidence of both low-birthweight and very low-birthweight babies) increased dramatically between 1986 and 1989 as a result of insufficient prenatal care, high-risk pregnancies, and substance abuse, especially crack cocaine.

All of this has placed a tremendous strain on the city's clinics and emergency rooms. The problems are further compounded by a severe shortage of office-based primary-care physicians. Seventy-four of ninety-six census tracts in Newark are designated as Primary Health Manpower Shortage areas.

In sum, it is clear, through any combination of economic, social, and health status indicators, that Newark ranks as one of the most troubled communities in the country.

Substance Abuse Treatment Programs

To develop a better understanding of the volume of treatment resources in Newark, as well as the characteristics of existing programs and whom they serve, we identified and conducted interviews with 23 organizations that appear to be the major providers of treatment within the city through the 54 individual programs that they administer. The most common type of program is the drug-free rehabilitation program. About half of these are residential (total capacity approximately 700) and half are outpatient (total capacity approximately 3,400) programs. In addition, there are four intensive day programs (total capacity approximately 165). There are also seven detoxification programs and two methadone maintenance programs (total capacity approximately 2,000) that primarily serve heroin users. The six aftercare and reentry programs in Newark have a combined capacity of about 400.

The majority of the programs surveyed were restricted to certain groups (e.g., age; gender; and special populations, such as AIDS patients, criminal justice cases, Spanish speakers, pregnant women, the homeless, and the mentally ill). There was only one special treatment program for the elderly, and very few programs were designed to accommodate women with young children.

Programs varied in terms of whether they were operating at, above, or below capacity, and most share their capacity with clients from outside of Newark. Other than the methadone programs, most did not specialize in substances, probably because of the high prevalence of polydrug use among their clientele.

Providers named inpatient detoxification, long-term residential rehabilitation, and intensive day programs as the treatment environments and modalities that had the greatest need for increased capacity. They agreed that women, especially pregnant women, were the group in greatest need of increased substance abuse treatment services and medical care; AIDS counseling and child care were named most frequently as the most important targets for increased collateral services for the treatment population.

While providers had many perspectives on what created the greatest barriers to obtaining treatment, the majority agreed that the most important barrier was the lack of adequate funding for indigent care. Other important barriers named had to do with the lack of outreach, especially identifying persons in need of treatment through the health, education, social service and criminal justice systems, and the logistical barriers that can present themselves in the course of applying to obtain treatment.

Substance Abuse Prevention Programs

Drug education is taught from kindergarten through twelfth grade in the Newark public schools. However, no empirical evaluation of Newark's classroom-based prevention education has been conducted. In addition, many organizations in Newark sponsor substance abuse education, intervention, and referral, but these efforts are not well coordinated on a citywide basis.

Drug Markets and Drug Dealing in Newark

To ascertain the character and pattern of drug dealing within Newark, and the characteristics of the dealers themselves, we conducted extensive interviews with 15 young men and women recently involved in drug selling in Newark and analyzed the prior records and dispositions of a sample of adults arrested for selling drugs by the Newark Police Department.

All of the people we interviewed, who at the time were in a juvenile correction facility or on probation, were younger than 26 years old. About half were working or had worked recently, but their attachments to the labor force were weak at best. Most had little education other than high school. Most of the males had prior drug arrests.

"Easy money" was the primary motivation for getting into drug selling. Typical gross income estimates ranged from $300 to $1200 per day, with a median of about $800. This probably represents net (untaxed) incomes of about $35 to $50 per hour, or $400 per day worked. This income was sufficient to support what was for them an opulent lifestyle. Most spent their money on jewelry, clothes, entertainment, and automobiles. Most said they were careful to avoid excessive drug use. Alcohol use was common among all sellers, but at low frequencies.

In contrast to the street markets in New York City neighborhoods, drug selling in Newark lacks formal organization; it is highly decentralized and entrepreneurial. There is little wholesale dealing. Young men who wish to enter the trade can set themselves up by purchasing small quantities of cocaine "wholesale" on the streets in New York and then can double their money by selling on street corners or in parks in Newark, in just a few days.

Cocaine is the most widely sold drug, and sellers depend on New York City suppliers for their product. Drug buyers seem to represent a wide cross section of working people in Newark—men and women, young and old, and from all social classes. Regular buyers generate the bulk of sellers' drug income.

The respondents reported that the risk of violence was considerable. Newark's cocaine market has spawned a secondary and apparently more violent robbery industry of "stickup boys": small crews of young men who specialize in robbing drug dealers. Most of the sellers had been robbed of their money or drugs at one time or another. Although all recognized the risks involved, none stopped selling because of the risks.

Our sample of arrested sellers consisted of 185 adults arrested for "selling drugs" or "possession with intent to sell" between July and December 1989. Sixty-five percent of the sample had prior adult arrests in New Jersey for drug offenses. Fifty-five percent had been arrested by Newark police for drugs.

Citywide, about half (54 percent) of those arrested were convicted of a felony, and 32 percent received a prison term. Arrestees from the target neighborhood were less likely to be convicted (one-third) or sent to prison if they were. The average prison term received was 48 months citywide and 43 months for those arrested from the target neighborhood.

Conclusion

Urban poverty and its associated ills of low educational attainment, high unemployment, inadequate housing, and high crime rates have long been endemic in a significant segment of the Newark community. In recent years, the problems of the chronic, long-term heroin users, half of whom have become HIV positive, and the epidemic of cocaine use that has swept the country have added to the ills that plague the city and many of its citizens. According to the available indicators from law enforcement and emergency room episodes, the recent decline in drug use evident at the metropolitan level was not evident for the city itself. Rather, alarming increases in the extent of heroin availability and use during 1990 heightened concerns that yet another dangerous epidemic may be in the making.

The data assembled for this study make it clear that many resources are already in place in Newark for dealing with the problems of substance abuse. But each of these resources—be it law enforcement activities, prevention, or substance abuse treatment—is targeted at a single aspect of the multifaceted problem. Further, there has been little coordination of services between one system, such as criminal justice, and another, for example, the treatment system. In addition, as the treatment providers we interviewed made clear, there are far too few resources available to meet the treatment and related needs of the indigent chronic substance abuser.

Our data also suggest that there is a great need for intervention with high risk groups, such as school-age youth and women of childbearing age, whose potential for extreme personal and social costs associated with substance abuse is greatest unless prevention and treatment resources are made available to them.

In Newark, the Fighting Back program has not taken a short-term view of the problems associated with substance abuse. Neither has it identified a single approach to fighting the problems, such as some enforcement and treatment efforts of the past have had. Instead, NFB recognizes the association between the long-existing problems of poverty that have produced dysfunctional families and neighborhoods and the added impact that drugs and alcohol abuse have made. NFB, and the many agencies and organizations that participate in it, is aimed at intervening in neighborhoods, in collaboration with government, private organizations, and neighborhood residents, to coordinate existing resources and broker additional resources that will strengthen families and neighborhoods and make them more drug resistant. This approach is intended to build on the already enormous potential of Newark citizens, the array of well-run programs already in place, and recent success in attracting a series of major residential, commercial, and educational development projects that can be expected to exert a positive influence on the neighborhoods in which they are located. NFB has adopted a positive approach, seeking to address underlying problems, and one that will be less bureaucratic and more flexible and sensitive to local needs than many that have preceded it.

Acknowledgments

This research could not have been conducted without the cooperation of the many officials and staff members of various public and private organizations in Newark and the state of New Jersey who gave generously of their time and data on behalf of this study. The staffs of the Newark city government, Board of Education, Newark Police Department, Newark Housing Authority, Essex County Division of Alcoholism and Drug Abuse, Essex County Prosecutor's Office, New Jersey Attorney General's Office, New Jersey State Police, New Jersey Division of Health, New Jersey Department of Corrections, and State Medical Examiner facilitated our data collection efforts. In addition, medical and treatment professionals and community leaders shared their expertise with us. We benefited immensely from their input and sincerely appreciate their cooperation.

We especially want to acknowledge the assistance of the many substance abuse treatment programs in the area for the cooperation of their personnel with our survey of substance-abuse treatment resources. And we thank Public Safety Electric and Gas Company (PSE&G) for making special computer runs to aid our research.

We would also like to acknowledge the contributions provided by the Fighting Back staff and the members of its various subcommittees—in particular, Boys' and Girls' Clubs of Newark President Barbara Wright Bell and Fighting Back Co-Chair Edwin H. Stier, who invited us to undertake this effort, and Fighting Back Project Director Irene James, with whom we worked closely throughout this study.

The study also benefited from the contributions of many colleagues at RAND and other institutions. We would like to thank Allan Abrahamse, Gary Bjork, Carol Edwards, Eva Feldman, Nora Fitzgerald, and Dan McCaffrey of RAND for their efforts on this project and also Gloria Tiwoni, a consultant to the project. We are also grateful to James Kahan of RAND and Ronald Ferguson of Harvard University, who provided helpful reviews of a draft of this report. Our secretarial staff, Roleana Trotter, Aimee Poquette, and Mary Sauters, provided outstanding project support. Thanks also to Peter Morrison for his advice on issues of residential mobility and to Peter Reuter and Barbara Williams, co-directors of RAND's Drug Policy Research Center for their advice and encouragement throughout the project.

1. Introduction

The Newark Fighting Back Initiative

Over the past two decades, the use of illegal drugs has increased sharply in the United States—as has the level of violence associated with their sale. Although the fraction of people reporting recent drug use and the recruitment of new users from the youthful population both appear to have declined since the mid-1980s, other indicators suggest that a large number of chronic users remain, causing serious negative consequences for themselves and their communities. In some areas, the effects of substance abuse and drug trafficking on families, neighborhoods, and social services have been particularly devastating, overwhelming the attempts of individuals and institutions to deal with them.

Newark, the largest city in New Jersey, is heavily affected by the host of problems associated with urban poverty and substance abuse. In 1989, The Boys' and Girls' Clubs of Newark received a two-year planning grant from the Robert Wood Johnson Foundation under the auspices of the foundation's national Fighting Back program. The purpose of the grant was to support the development of a comprehensive community-based plan for reducing substance abuse in selected neighborhoods.

The Newark Fighting Back (NFB) Initiative is a community development effort that seeks to identify existing community strengths; build capacity within the community to manage constructive change; and empower the community to stimulate values that will not tolerate dysfunctional behaviors and that will support the recovery process.[1]

The NFB effort has two primary objectives:

1. Build the capacity of grass-roots organizations (tenant associations, block watch groups, neighborhood coalitions, etc.) to participate in community problem solving; and

---

[1]Although The Boys' and Girls' Clubs of Newark is the lead agency for the effort, the mayor of Newark is the honorary chairman. The four co-chairs during the developmental period included the congressional representative from the area, the city's business administrator, a former attorney general, and a former director of the New Jersey Division of Criminal Justice. Officials from many relevant treatment, prevention, education, social service, law enforcement, correction, and private-sector agencies were represented on a number of consortium committees, each focusing on a particular aspect of the problem.

2. Working through the consortium committees, coordinate the development of a comprehensive human services system to support the work of the neighborhood coalitions.

Most of the NFB efforts during the planning grant period focused on the problems of citizens residing within a 72-square-block neighborhood in Newark's Central Ward.[2] This target area was selected to serve as a prototype for subsequent community development efforts to be conducted in other parts of the city.

The principal law enforcement element during the planning grant period was Operation Homestead, which included the establishment of a police substation on the ground floor of a large, run-down apartment building near the center of the target neighborhood; an increase in the number of officers assigned to the target neighborhood, including a complement of state troopers who worked in tandem with Newark police officers; and increased use of foot patrol and community problem-solving by the beefed-up contingent of city and state police.

Overview of the RAND Needs Assessment

In December 1990, The Boys' and Girls' Clubs of Newark commissioned RAND to perform a needs assessment for its Fighting Back effort. The purpose of the assessment was to provide the NFB planning effort with quantitative information and analysis of the extent and characteristics of drug problems and the existing resources and capacity to respond to these problems. Since there has never been a citywide epidemiological survey of drug use in Newark, no data were available for directly measuring the prevalence or extent of illegal substance abuse and its consequences among the general population. Lacking epidemiological survey data, we analyzed instead a number of *indicators* of substance abuse problems and consequences, including arrests for drug offenses and morbidity and mortality data. To supplement these data, we interviewed several key informants in health, education, law enforcement, and other social service professions. We also surveyed treatment program providers to learn more about the features of their programs, the populations they serve, and the nature and size of their caseloads.

Finally, to develop a picture of the marketing and distribution of drugs in Newark, we interviewed a small number of recently arrested dealers.

---

[2]The area extends three to five blocks north and south of Spruce Street and six blocks west and one block east of Martin Luther King Boulevard. A map appears in Section 2.

Organization of This Report

The next section of this report provides background information on Newark and the Fighting Back target neighborhood identified during the NFB planning grant period. This information includes history, demographics, employment, income, trends in crime and other social problem indicators, and residential stability. In Section 3, we set the context for Newark's drug problems with a brief look at national trends in drug abuse and then describe the situation in Newark and the target neighborhood, as reflected by a number of substance abuse indicators. Section 4 describes the drug treatment and prevention resources currently available within the community, noting some of the areas where additional resources might be used most effectively. Section 5 contains information on drug dealing in the city collected through interviews with 15 young dealers arrested for selling drugs in Newark. It also includes an analysis of the prior records and dispositions for a sample of adults arrested for drug selling. Section 6 presents our conclusions and some recommendations for easing the impact of substance abuse on Newark.

2. Conditions in Newark and a Fighting Back Target Neighborhood

Newark

Patterns of drug use and trafficking and other types of crime do not just occur randomly. They are more likely to occur within particular population groups that are also at high risk for a number of social problems or problem behaviors, including early school dropout, teen pregnancy, and chronic unemployment (Greenwood, 1992). These patterns are also more likely to occur in areas exhibiting certain conducive conditions, such as high rates of poverty and broken homes, neighborhood disorganization and decline, and easy transportation access to major commercial markets (Skogan, 1990).

Although a large fraction of the population and several areas of Newark currently exhibit many of these risk factors, the situation was not always so bleak. At times in its recent past, the city has been a bustling Mecca for industry and commerce. To understand Newark's current drug problems, we must begin with a brief review of its history and population trends.

History[1]

The city of Newark was founded on the banks of the Passaic River in the spring of 1666 by a small band of Puritans from Milford, Connecticut. During the century following its founding, Newark became noted for its quarries and the manufacturing of harnesses, cider, coach lace, and shoes. The completion of two bridges in 1790 changed Newark from an off-the-beaten-track village into a bustling center of commerce. The rise of huge factories between 1870 and 1900 gave the city economic diversity. In the 1920s, the downtown area began building upward in imitation of the New York skyline across the river. A new airport and a new seaport brought links to international markets and ideas.

During the 1950s and 1960s, Newark's steadily dwindling white majority resisted the political demands of the city's rapidly increasing black and Hispanic population (as the Puritans had resisted the demands of other "freemen" 250

---

[1]Based on Cunningham (1988).

years earlier) for better access to jobs, housing, and political power. In the summer of 1967, festering resentment over these and other perceived injustices combined with a sweltering heat wave to produce several nights of rioting in the black community. Acting on a formal request from the city's mayor, the governor sent in the State Police and National Guard to restore order. A number of citizens were killed when these troops fired at what they thought were snipers in residential buildings. Altogether, 26 people were killed in the riots.

Although parts of the city are still struggling to recover from the devastation of the riot, and the neglect that preceded it, other parts of the city have undergone extensive commercial and residential development over the last several years.

The Newark "Renaissance" effort, a coalition of community and business interests, has produced the state's largest office complex (Gateway Center); new cultural, educational, and corporate facilities (such as the PSE&G headquarters building); and growth in private housing development. New employers have been attracted to the city recently, including a major U.S. Postal Service facility, and the expansion of the Newark International Airport has increased employment opportunities.

Demographics

Newark is the largest city in New Jersey, with 275,221 residents.[2] Figure 2.1 shows how the city compares in size with several of the other large cities in New Jersey (as of 1988), other northeastern cities with comparable demographics, nearby East Coast cities, and U.S. cities to which it seems most similar.[3] In terms of population, Newark is the 49th largest city in the United States.

The city occupies 24.1 square miles and is part of the greater New York City metropolitan area. It is located only 20 minutes by Port Authority Trans-Hudson (PATH) train from The World Trade Center and only minutes from Jersey City, the second largest city in the state.

Newark is located in Essex County, which had a population of 778,206 in 1990. The city is part of a Primary Metropolitan Statistical Area (PMSA) that includes Essex, Morris, Sussex, and Union counties. Newark's population has a number of characteristics that are usually associated with high rates of drug use and other behavioral problems. Newark is also the third fastest-shrinking city in the

[2]1990 U.S. Census data.
[3]Data for this same group of cities will be presented in several subsequent figures as a way of putting the demographic characteristics of Newark in perspective.

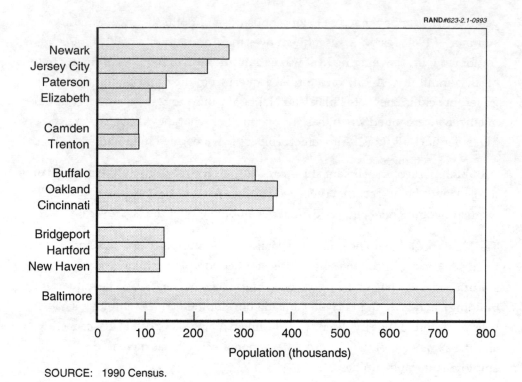

SOURCE: 1990 Census.

Figure 2.1—Population of Newark Compared with Other Cities

country (after Gary, Indiana, and Youngstown, Ohio), losing 16 percent of its population between 1980 and 1990. Figure 2.2 shows the pattern of population change for Newark and several other cities.

In 1990, Newark's population was 71 percent non-white, while the rest of Essex county was 37 percent non-white, and the rest of the PMSA was 30 percent non-white. The black population decreased from 207,458 in 1970 to 191,743 in 1980 and 160,885 in 1990; however, between 1980 and 1990, the black population remained at 58 percent of the total population. The white population decreased only slightly, from 30.8 percent in 1980 to 28.6 percent in 1990. The Hispanic population increased over the last decade from 18.6 to 26.1 percent of the total population in 1990. Figure 2.3 shows how Newark's racial composition compares to several other cities. Table 2.1 shows the racial distribution of the city of Newark, for 1990.

The Newark PMSA also has a large immigrant population, with an estimated 10,041 immigrants admitted in 1988, the thirteenth highest number among

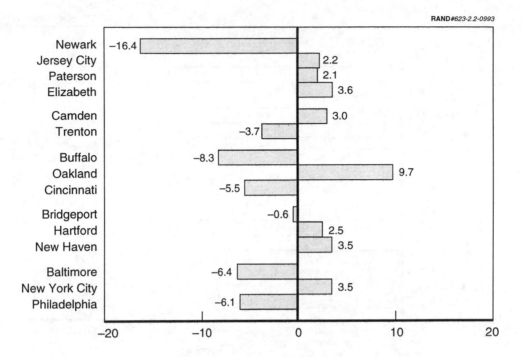

SOURCE: 1980 and 1990 Census.

Figure 2.2—Population Change in Newark and Comparison Cities

PMSAs in the United States. The largest number of immigrants to the Newark area in 1988 came from Haiti, totaling 1,337.[4]

Census figures released in 1990 show that 52.2 percent of Newark's population is female. About 30 percent of the population is under 18 years old, and 9 percent is 65 and older. Table 2.1 shows the age breakdown of the population by race and gender.

According to the 1990 Census, the school-age population of Newark live in a variety of household types with only about one-third living in married-couple households. Forty-four percent live in single-parent households. Seventeen percent live with relatives other than parents, and another four percent live in group quarters or with nonrelatives.

---

[4]U.S. Department of Commerce (1990), p. 10.

8

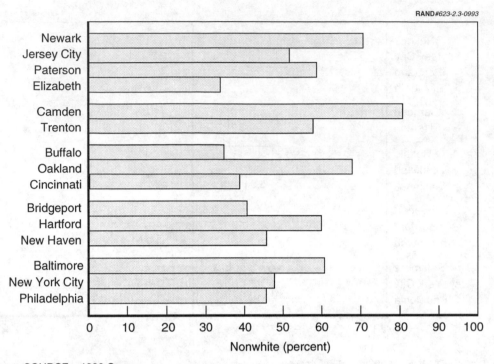

RAND#623-2.3-0993

SOURCE: 1990 Census.

Figure 2.3—Racial Composition of Newark and Comparison Cities

Employment and Income

The recent national economic recession has seriously affected employment in the Newark metropolitan area. Table 2.2 shows unemployment rates for the Newark PMSA from 1986 through 1990. Blacks and Hispanics, who together constitute 82 percent of Newark's population, have experienced the greatest recent increases in unemployment.

In addition, prospects for employment growth in this region of New Jersey are lower than for elsewhere in the state. A labor market analysis of the Newark area produced by the Newark Mayor's Office of Employment and Training in October 1990 reported the expectation of increased jobs in construction in the short term, but the analysis suggested that the greatest growth is likely to be in such areas as health services, which typically require extensive education and technical training. Several industries, which require lower skills, were expected to continue to decline in Newark.

The high rate of unemployment and the low-skilled jobs held by many Newark residents combine to produce extremely low levels of per capita income in

Table 2.1

Newark Population, 1990: Persons by Age, Race, and Sex

Age Breakdown	White		Black		Asian or Pacific Islander		Other Race		Hispanic Origin of Any Race	
	Total	% Female	Total	% Female	Total	% Female	Total	% Female	Total	% Female
School age										
5–11	6,953	50	18,523	49	256	46	4,391	49	9,211	49
12–14	3,024	49	7,787	50	91	56	1,907	50	3,862	49
15–17	3,134	47	8,302	48	116	50	1,891	47	3,882	46
Working and voting age										
16+	62,894	50	118,231	55	2,670	49	22,024	50	50,897	50
16–64	51,399	48	105,349	54	2,532	49	20,993	50	47,476	49
18+	60,601	51	112,616	55	2,584	49	19,749	54	48,253	50
18–64	49,306	48	99,734	54	2,446	49	19,695	50	44,832	50
Other age groups										
0–4	4,859	48	13,657	50	234	45	3,368	49	6,553	50
5–17	13,111	49	34,612	49	463	49	8,189	48	16,955	48
18–44	33,789	47	71,817	53	1,986	48	15,529	51	34,184	49
45–64	15,517	50	27,917	57	460	50	4,166	53	10,648	51
62+	13,745	60	16,248	61	179	53	1,062	57	4,451	57
65+	11,495	62	12,882	62	138	51	1,032	57	3,421	59
Total all ages	78,771	50	160,885	54	3,281	49	32,284	50	71,761	50

SOURCE: Preliminary 1990 Census, STF1, P12.

Table 2.2

Trends in Unemployment in the Newark PMSA

	Percent Unemployed				
	1986	1987	1988	1989	1990
PMSA TOTAL	5.3	4.4	3.9	4.7	6.4
Men	5.0	4.3	3.9	5.1	7.0
Women	5.7	4.4	3.9	4.2	5.6
Black	10.7	10.5	8.8	9.3	12.2
Men	11.3	11.0	9.0	8.9	12.6
Women	10.1	10.0	8.7	9.7	11.7
Hispanic	7.1	6.4	5.0	5.4	9.1
Men	5.5	6.8	5.0	4.9	11.7
Women	9.4	7.3	5.0	5.5	5.7
White	4.1	3.1	2.7	3.6	4.8
Men	3.8	3.2	2.8	4.1	5.6
Women	4.6	3.0	2.5	2.0	3.7

SOURCE: U.S. Bureau of Labor Statistics.

Newark. Income data from the 1990 Census show Newark per capita income at $10,509, among the lowest for urban locations in the U.S.

One-third of the population is eligible for Medicaid, and almost 30 percent have received aid to dependent children (French, June 1990). Figures 2.4 and 2.5 show that, compared to similar cities, a high percentage of Newark's population lives below the poverty level and in female-headed households.

AIDS and Other Public Health Problems

Newark has the highest number of adult and pediatric Acquired Immuno-deficiency Syndrome (AIDS) cases of any city in New Jersey. According to data from the AIDS Data Analysis Unit, New Jersey Department of Health, 2,233 cases of AIDS had been reported in Newark as of April 1991. Excluding pediatric cases, 69 percent involved intravenous (IV) drug users. The proportion of adult AIDS cases with heterosexual activity as the only risk factor is increasing rapidly, currently accounting for about 10 percent of all cases. Other evidence suggests a higher rate; the December 1991 Community Epidemiology Working Group (CEWG) Newark report states that "Since October 31, 1989, heterosexual transmission has been responsible for 18 percent of new adult cases" (French, December 1991, p. 196).

Twenty-nine percent of all adult cases are female. An article in the December 16, 1990, edition of *The New York Times* referred to a survey at a Newark hospital in

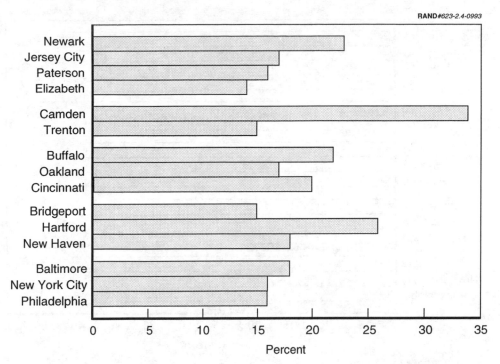

RAND#623-2.4-0993

SOURCE: 1990 Census.

Figure 2.4—Families Below Poverty Level in Newark and Comparison Cities

1988 that found that 1 of every 23 babies born there is born to a mother with the human immunodeficiency virus (HIV). Blacks are overrepresented among AIDS cases in Newark, accounting for 86 percent of adult cases and 76 percent of pediatric cases; Hispanics account for 10 percent, and whites for 5 percent. Appendix E provides a summary of the AIDS caseload in Newark in 1991. From these data, French concluded that "AIDS in Newark continues to be concentrated among IV drug users and their sex partners in the minority community." (French, 1991b, p. 193).

Other health indicators also reflect a severe and troubled environment. Among all of the cities in New Jersey, Newark has the highest number of low-birthweight babies and births among adolescents; the highest number of infant, neonatal, and postneonatal deaths; and the highest number of syphilis, gonorrhea, and clinically active tuberculosis cases.

Newark also has a high rate of teen pregnancy. While the exact number of teen pregnancies cannot be determined, the number of live births to unwed mothers eighteen and under was 979 in 1987 and 945 in 1988.[5] In 1988, 93 percent of

_____

[5]Data for more recent years are not yet available.

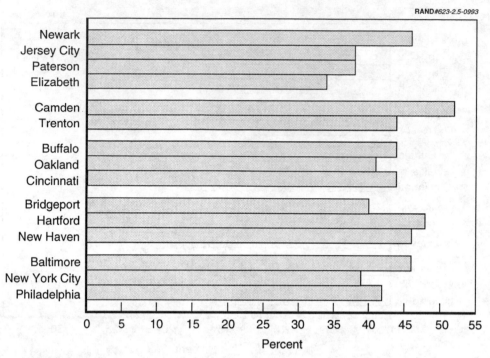

SOURCE: 1990 Census.

**Figure 2.5—Percentage of Female-Headed Households in Newark
and Comparison Cities**

births to teens were to unwed mothers, representing 15 percent of all live births
in Newark that year, a rate higher than in most cities with populations over
100,000 (Vital Statistics of the United States, 1990). Assuming the preliminary
1990 census figures on female age distribution applied in 1988, children were
born that year to approximately 10 percent of the female high-school–age
population in Newark. Comparisons among the 75 largest U.S. cities in 1980
showed that Newark had the highest percentage of births to mothers under 20
years old.

The city also saw a dramatic increase in premature births (the incidence of both
low-birthweight and very low-birthweight babies) between 1986 and 1989.
According to congressional testimony by Bernard Dickens, Sr., president of the
United Hospitals Medical Center in Newark, this extremely expensive health
care problem in Newark results from insufficient prenatal care, high-risk
pregnancies, and substance abuse, especially crack cocaine.

It is likely that the pervasive presence of crime, poverty, and drugs has had a
negative impact on the mental well-being of many of the city's youth. One recent
study certainly indicates this. Researchers at the New Jersey College of Medicine

and Dentistry conducted a survey of healthy adolescents 12 to 22 years old who were attending an inner city medical clinic in Newark between November 1987 and April 1988. They found a total lifetime prevalence rate for major depressive disorders (MDD) of 30 percent among those surveyed, many of whom reported recurrent episodes.[6] The rate of stressful life events among the population surveyed was quite high, with 17 percent reporting that one or both parents had died, 50 percent that they had witnessed violence, and 8 percent that they had been a victim of sexual abuse.

All of these health problems, coupled with the drug-related emergency room episodes, have placed a tremendous strain on the city's clinics and emergency rooms. Emergency rooms report repeated temporary closures because of overload conditions, as well as long waits for ambulatory patients. The problems are further compounded by a severe shortage of office-based primary-care physicians, which results in further demands on emergency rooms for care of nonemergency patients. Seventy-four of ninety-six census tracts in Newark are designated as Primary Health Manpower Shortage areas.

Crime

According to the FBI's Uniform Crime Reports (UCR), Newark has one of the highest per capita crime rates in the country, with 14,331 index offenses per 100,000 population reported in 1989, compared to a national average of 5,741.[7] Newark's crime rate has been rising rapidly over the last 5 years, increasing by 41 percent between 1984 and 1989; during this same period, the nationwide UCR rate increased by only 14 percent. Within specific crime types, Newark has particularly high rates of homicide, robbery, and auto theft. Homicide and robbery rates for Newark and several comparison cities are shown in Figures 2.6 and 2.7.

It is commonly believed that the recent upsurge in the cocaine and crack trade has led to increases in violence as dealers compete with one another for turf; "stickup boys" rob street dealers; and buyers or dealers retaliate against each other for deals gone sour. In Newark, while the number of homicides per year has been steadily declining for at least the last 10 years, between 1986 and 1988 the fraction of homicides identified as drug-related by the Newark Police

---

[6] The paper presenting the results of the survey (Bartlett, et al., 1991) raises the issue of the representativeness of the survey sample and points out the possibility that this group could be either more or less subject to MDD than community-based populations.

[7] UCR index offenses include murder, forcible rape, robbery, aggravated assault, burglary, larceny-theft, and motor vehicle theft.

14

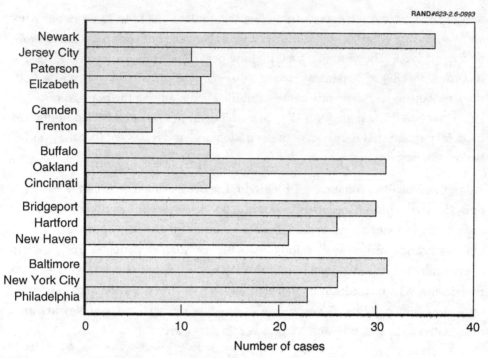

RAND#623-2.6-0993

SOURCE: 1988 Uniform Crime Reports (UCR).

Figure 2.6—Homicides per 100,000 Population in Newark and Comparison Cities

Department increased by more than a factor of 4—escalating from 2 percent to 9 percent of all cases.[8]

School Dropout Rates

One more social problem that usually goes hand-in-hand with high poverty and crime rates is school dropout. Annual secondary school dropout rates in Newark increased during the 1980s until the 1987–88 school year, when they reached a peak of 11 percent then dropped to 9.3 percent in 1989–90. Most of this decline is accounted for by changes in one school, Central High School, which serves the NFB target neighborhood. The dropout rate at this school declined significantly from 20.5 percent schoolwide in 1988–89 to 8.9 percent in 1989–90. This decline is attributed to a change in school administration at Central High School and to outreach efforts put in place by the Cluster Schools Program to prepare eighth graders for the transition to high school.

---

[8]The national average has been estimated to be around 10 percent, with considerable variation across cities (Reiss and Roth, 1993).

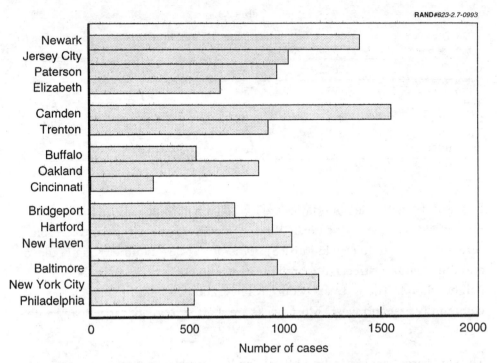

RAND#623-2.7-0993

SOURCE: 1988 UCR.

Figure 2.7—Robberies per 100,000 Population in Newark and Comparison Cities

Table 2.3 shows the dropout rate by grade for the past several years. It is clear that the greatest at-risk grades are 9th and 11th. Dropout among special education students is also high and has been increasing over the last few years. The available data do not allow precise estimates of dropout rates for class cohorts; however, after excluding those who transfer among school districts, they do facilitate rough estimates. For example, tracking the dropout rate from Newark high schools for an entering cohort in Fall 1986, we found that, assuming the group remained within the Newark public school system, as many as 38 percent would have dropped out by June of 1990.[9]

Newark Fighting Back Target Neighborhood

The neighborhood that NFB targeted during its planning-grant phase is located for the most part in the city's central ward, to the south of the downtown

---

[9]Given the decrease in population of the city over the last decade, it is likely that a significant number of students leave the Newark school system during secondary school and continue their schooling in some other school district. Some of those who left may be counted by mistake as dropouts rather than transfers.

Table 2.3
Newark Secondary Schools Dropout Rates

Grade	1987	1988	1989	1990
Ninth	10.9	13.4	11.9	8.8
Tenth	9.3	9.5	10.1	8.9
Eleventh	11.6	10.3	10.5	10.7
Twelfth	8.0	8.5	9.4	7.6
Special Ed.	9.1	12.5	13.8	13.6

SOURCE: Newark Board of Education.

business district. The boundaries are Irvine Turner Boulevard on the west, Springfield Avenue on the north, Washington Street on the east, and Clinton Avenue on the south (see Figure 2.8). Other than Martin Luther King Boulevard and the boundary streets, no through streets run north or south in the neighborhood. Three streets (Court, Kinney, and Spruce) run through the community east and west. Most blocks are short and do not carry heavy auto traffic.

The small area east of Martin Luther King Boulevard is in the east ward. The neighborhood falls within three zip codes, three census tracts, and two police sectors. Zip, census tract, and sector boundaries extend beyond the boundaries of the target neighborhood, making it impossible to describe the characteristics of the target neighborhood population exclusively. However, because the immediately surrounding neighborhoods appear to be quite similar, we present statistics about the neighborhood using total zip code, census tract, and police sector data, as available.

The target neighborhood was once among the most exclusive in Newark. Many mansions were built in this district, formerly known as "the hill," because of its commanding view of the river. Several of these mansions are still standing and are being used as schools and other institutions. Others are undergoing renovation. Today, this area is among the poorest and least advantaged in the city. Much of the housing is old, including multistory and single-family buildings. Two major high-rise public housing projects are located in the neighborhood, as well as a large number of Housing and Urban Development Section 8 subsidized housing units. Other housing includes newer public housing low-rise and town-house developments and a large low-rise cooperative, known as High Park Gardens. There is one large complex with housing for seniors. There are several vacant lots throughout the neighborhood, concentrated near the Stella Wright and Edward Scudder public housing projects. About 20 percent of the blocks in the area are totally vacant.

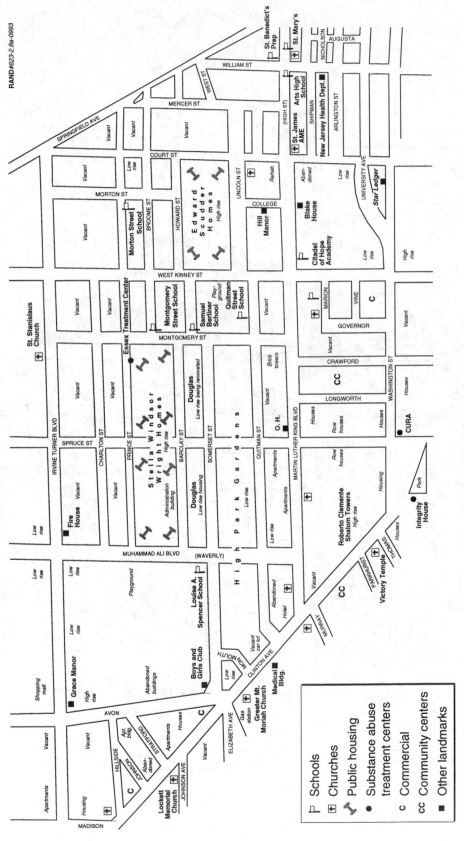

Figure 2.8a—Fighting Back Target Neighborhood

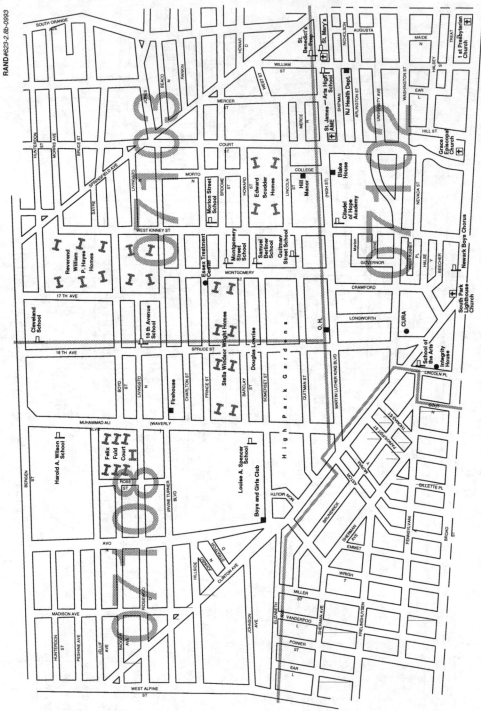

Figure 2.8b—Fighting Back Target Neighborhood and Surrounding Area

RAND#6023-2.8b-0993

The area contains very little commercial development, except on the Clinton Avenue boundary. There is only one large business in the area, the *Star-Ledger* newspaper, located on the northeast boundary of the neighborhood. There are, however, a number of schools, churches, and community organizations within or on the boundaries of the neighborhood. There are a number of medical clinics, and just north of the area is a large acute care hospital. In the southern portion of the neighborhood there is a Boys' and Girls' Club and a large playground and playing-field area. There is one fire station within the boundaries.

The Newark Police Department's Operation Homestead, which began on November 26, 1990, is headquartered at 725 Martin Luther King Boulevard (at the intersection of Martin Luther King Boulevard and Spruce). Newark was the fourth city in New Jersey to implement such a joint neighborhood policing effort between local and state police. A memorandum from the Police Director at the time listed the following goals of the effort:

1. Organize the community

2. Drive out drug dealers

3. Discourage drug customers from coming to the neighborhood

4. Stabilize the neighborhood so that the police can phase out their intense coverage and the community can assert its control over the neighborhood.[10]

At one point, the program involved as many as 33 state troopers in addition to Newark Police Department personnel and several undercover Sheriff's Narcotic Unit officers. The program has not focused on massive arrests, but rather on deterring drug sales and related crime in the area and on assisting residents in reclaiming the neighborhood.

According to a report by the Police Foundation (Sheppard and Pate, 1991) which evaluated the program, the presence of the officers in the neighborhood was immediately noticeable to residents. Residents and many others who know the area noticed that the impact on dealing was also immediate, with the blatant street dealing disappearing from the Martin Luther King–Spruce intersection. When they began, the foot patrols in the area were expected to continue for several months.

---

[10]Coleman (1990).

Demographics

We have used preliminary 1990 census data on total population by census block to estimate a population of about 15,875 in the target neighborhood, or about 6 percent of the total Newark population. The neighborhood's rate of population decline (about 40 percent over the past decade) exceeds that of the city. Much of the decline is due to demolition of high-rise public housing buildings in the area and the relocation of public housing residents during building renovation. The neighborhood is predominantly black, with 2 percent of the households occupied by whites and 4 percent by Hispanics.

Other 1990 Census data at the block and tract level were not yet available at the time of our study. Several characteristics of the 1980 population for the census tracts that include the target neighborhood are shown in Table 2.4.

Overall, it appears that the neighborhood population had slightly more females of childbearing age than the city as a whole, a higher fertility rate among these women, and a higher percentage of the total population under age 18. While the city as a whole has a large percentage of children living with single parents, the rate is even higher in the target neighborhood. Almost everyone, 96 percent, lived in rental housing. While the population in this neighborhood is a fairly stable one, as discussed in the following section, some of the characteristics shown in Table 2.5 may have changed significantly over the past ten years as some of the high-rise buildings with large apartments for families have been torn down.

Residential Stability

According to 1980 Census figures, as many as 60 percent of the population over five years old in the target neighborhood had lived in their residences for five

Table 2.4

Demographics of Census Tracts Containing Target Neighborhood (percent)

Persons under 18	35
Persons 65+	9
Female among persons 15+	59
Fertility rate (women aged 15–44)	1.81
Under 18 living in single-parent households	59
White households	2
Households of Hispanic origin	4
Persons in rental housing	96

SOURCE: 1980 U.S. Census, *Characteristics of Households and Families.*

years or more. This was slightly higher than the rate for the city as a whole, which was 57 percent at the time.

Data on length of residence were not available from the 1990 Census, but we were able to obtain additional information from utility company records, which show the dates that residential accounts are opened. Public Safety Electric and Gas Company (PSE&G) provided us with this information for a sample of residential addresses within the target neighborhood. The sample was limited to individual meter accounts and thus excluded all of the public housing units and much of the subsidized housing, which are on master meters.

The utility records, current as of 1991, show that the neighborhood is still quite stable, with 52 percent of the accounts opened more than five years ago. Thirty-six percent were opened 10 or more years ago. Only 12.6 percent of the 231 addresses we examined had opened utility accounts within the last twelve months. Comparing this information with that of the American Housing Survey, which includes Newark, shows that the target neighborhood appears to have slightly fewer recent move-ins than the rest of Newark.

Other evidence also suggests that much of the population of the neighborhood consists of long-term residents. Tenants in the neighborhood's Section 8 buildings, when discussing housing problems, reported that they had lived for many years in their buildings. Public housing authority representatives told us that, because waiting lists for public housing units are so long and alternative housing in the neighborhood is so hard to get, public housing tenants are also mostly long-term residents.

There is no physical evidence of single-room occupancy hotels or other boarding houses or short-term residency housing in the target neighborhood. However, we heard from some long-term tenants that one of their concerns is landlords who rent to transient drug dealers.

3. Substance Abuse in Newark

Introduction

In the previous section, we described numerous demographic and socioeconomic conditions in Newark that make it a high-risk community for substance abuse problems. But with the exception of information that directly links drug abuse to AIDS cases, we cannot causally link drug abuse to the many other problems Newark faces. In this section, we examine direct indicators of substance abuse problems in the city and in the target neighborhood. Where possible, we compare Newark and other major metropolitan areas.

Only a limited analysis of the nature and extent of Newark's substance abuse problems can be undertaken with the existing indicators. Comprehensive epidemiological data describing the number of users and the consequences they suffer do not exist for Newark. National numbers have little utility here, because the characteristics of the community are markedly different from those of the national population. Even data collected at the state level do not provide a detailed picture for Newark.

What do exist are several diverse indicators of substance abuse problems in Newark and the NFB target neighborhood, such as health consequences, deaths, arrests, community perceptions, and admissions to treatment. From these totally unintegrated systems, we can describe the populations that experience the consequences monitored by each. We cannot, however, provide a comprehensive analysis of drug abuse consequences, and we cannot describe the larger drug-using populations that do not experience the consequences monitored.

Before turning to the local indicators, we provide a brief overview of the rise of heroin and cocaine abuse nationwide and discuss the limitations of the available data.

National Trends in Drug Abuse[1]

The rise and spread of heroin and cocaine among inner-city communities appears to be primarily a post–World War II phenomenon. Prior to World War II, heroin use was essentially confined to a few large cities. Only about 20 percent of those arrested on drug charges were black. By the mid-1950s, the percentage had grown to over 50 percent.

World War II brought thousands of southern blacks and Puerto Ricans to the New York area to fill wartime industrial jobs. Largely because of patterns in housing discrimination, most settled in inner-city white ethnic neighborhoods, a pattern of migration that continued after the war up through the 1960s. Most of these first-generation migrants succeeded in finding employment and avoided the drug abuse that was to later affect their children.

In the mid-1950s, sizable numbers of white and minority inner-city youths in New York and Los Angeles began to use heroin and became addicted to the drug. The heroin that was available on the street became heavily adulterated, and most frequent users progressed from "snorting" (nasal inhalation) and "skin-popping" (injection under the skin) to "mainlining" (injection into a vein). By 1960, a heroin-injection subculture had become institutionalized in New York, Chicago, and Los Angeles, but was rare in other metropolitan areas.

During the late 1960s, marijuana use exploded across the country in concert with the rapidly expanding civil rights, counterculture, and antiwar movements. While only 5 percent of U.S. high school seniors had used marijuana in the previous 12 months in 1965, the percentage had climbed to 30 percent by 1970, and to 49 percent by 1980.

Heroin use and addiction, particularly among minorities in inner-city neighborhoods, also increased dramatically during the late 1960s. Most heroin users began use between the ages of 15 and 21, and many became addicted within one to two years.

The "heroin generation" that became addicted in the late 1960s and early 1970s is evident today in the black community in virtually every moderate to large size city. Estimates of its size range from 800,000 to several million. Many of this generation entered the detoxification, drug-free, or methadone treatment programs established during this era and remain the major population group being treated for opiate addiction. The average age of opiate users in treatment

---

[1]This section is largely based on Johnson et al. (1990).

was in the mid-thirties by 1990. The heroin users from this generation are largely polydrug abusers who use on a daily basis or several times a week. Many like to heat cocaine and heroin together and inject the mixture as a "speedball."

As the heroin epidemic began to ease in the mid-1970s, cocaine snorting became increasingly popular among non-heroin users in the inner city. During this period, cocaine became known as a "status drug" that was relatively harmless to the user.

By the late 1970s, a new technique for purifying adulterated cocaine, called "freebasing," emerged in Los Angeles. When the cocaine is heated at low temperature and its fumes are inhaled, the freebase provides the user with an almost immediate euphoric high, which lasts about 20 minutes, followed by a rapid dysphoria, in which the user feels worse than usual.

The first seizures by authorities of rock cocaine (crack) occurred in Los Angeles in 1984, to be quickly followed by its appearance in New York. Although crack use exploded during 1986 and 1987 in many major cities, where it became the predominant drug, crack has never been very popular in Newark, where powder cocaine remains the form in which the drug is most readily available.

In most areas of the country, the number of recent users and the rate of new users of cocaine began to decline after peaking around 1985, as indicated by self-report surveys (such as the National Household Survey on Drug Abuse and the High School Senior Survey). However, the federally sponsored Drug Abuse Warning Network (DAWN), which collects data on drug-related emergency room admissions and drug-related deaths, and the Drug Use Forecasting Program (DUF), which monitors drug use among arrestees, have not shown similar trends among the populations they monitor. One possible explanation for the different patterns is that, while recreational use is down, chronic cocaine use and its consequences continue among high-risk populations, such as arrestees.

Sources and Limitations of Newark Drug Data

The data sources that are typically used for generating estimates of substance use or abuse for any given population are self-report surveys (household surveys for adults and school-administered surveys for juveniles) and random drug testing (systematically done for arrestees in some cities under DUF). Unfortunately, none of these sources is available for Newark. There has never been a citywide epidemiological survey of drug use, comparable to the National Household

Survey on Drug Abuse, and the present study did not include such an effort.[2] The New Jersey Department of Law and Public Safety conducts a periodic survey of New Jersey high school students, which includes students from Newark high schools; but the results of this study are only generalizable to the statewide high-school population, and to urban and rural high-school populations.[3] Other surveys that have obtained information about the rate of drug use among special youth populations have problems of sample bias and lack of generalizability.

Newark does have several sources of data for monitoring the consequences of drug use. Newark is one of 21 metropolitan areas around the country that participate in the DAWN, in which Newark hospital emergency rooms and county medical examiners provide data on drug-related hospital visits and deaths. Arrests for drug offenses by the Newark Police Department (NPD) provide another useful indicator. State and local databases on the substance abuse treatment population provide information about who is obtaining such treatment. Newark is also one of several municipalities around the country that participate in the CEWG; this group produces regular summaries of the patterns of drug use in each of the participating cities.

Each of these sources helps to form a picture of drug use problems. Yet, each is subject to limitations and may actually distort the picture. For example, we can determine the number of arrests in the police department sectors that cover the target neighborhood and compare those with the rest of the city. More specifically, data on arrests for possession or sale of drugs give us useful information about the availability of different drugs in different parts of the city. But levels and targets of law enforcement activity greatly affect these numbers. Furthermore, arrests alone do not indicate drug use among arrestees.

The DAWN data on drug-related emergency room episodes and drug-related deaths provide important information about the characteristics of the population that suffers serious consequences from drug abuse. However, the conclusions that can be drawn from these data are also subject to certain limitations. Obviously, only a portion of drug abusers visit emergency rooms or die as a direct result of drug abuse. In some locations, there are also alternative sources of medical care for drug emergencies during daytime hours.

Among low socioeconomic-status population groups in the inner city, emergency room care in public hospitals may be the only option for health care. As poverty

---

[2]Several years ago, a survey of the New Jersey household population was undertaken, which included a subsample representative of Northern New Jersey, but not Newark.

[3]Results from this youth survey are presented later in this section.

and unemployment increase, greater portions of the population may use emergency rooms than in previous years, distorting the trends we observe in drug abuse episodes.

It is important to note that emergency room episodes distort much of the pattern of substance use in the community. For example, although marijuana is widely used, recreational use of marijuana and other drugs is not likely to result in acute or chronic symptoms requiring emergency room visits. In addition, alcohol alone is not captured by the DAWN system. On the other hand, because the combined use of several drugs, especially in combination with alcohol, can be very toxic, the likely result is emergency room visits at rates higher than the overall use rate in the community. Thus, DAWN data may tend to exaggerate or inflate the frequency of polydrug use, in comparison to heavy use of one drug or alcohol alone.

Finally, younger people are better able to metabolize drug ingredients than older people, which also affects whose usage is captured in emergency room episodes. It may even be true that females have greater access to emergency room care than do males, because of Medicaid insurance benefits, which are directly linked to welfare status. In sum, DAWN data are extremely complex, and their accurate interpretation is difficult.

One must also use care in interpreting the data on Newark's substance abuse treatment programs. Data about those in treatment are not necessarily representative of the larger substance-abusing population or the population in need of treatment, but not receiving it. The size and nature of the treatment population are partly functions of treatment referral sources and partly functions of the slots available for specific populations and/or conditions.

Surveys of New Jersey High School Students

The New Jersey Department of Law and Public Safety has periodically conducted surveys of New Jersey high school students regarding their use of drugs. A comparison of responses to the 1980, 1986, and 1989 surveys shows a considerable decline in drug use among this population (Fisher, 1990). Youth still in school are using remarkably fewer drugs and are perceiving drug use as much more dangerous. (This is probably not the case for those who have dropped out of school.) Lifetime prevalence rates for all drugs and alcohol among this group have steadily declined (see Table 3.1), although the decline for alcohol is much smaller than that for drugs. Annual prevalence rates have also declined (see Table 3.2).

Table 3.1

Lifetime Prevalence for New Jersey High School Students
(percentage ever used)

Drug	1980	1986	1989
Alcohol	91.2	89.2	83.9
Marijuana	61.4	49.0	32.1
Hallucinogens	15.8	13.0	9.8
Cocaine	16.6	19.2	9.4

SOURCE: Fisher (1990).

Table 3.2

Annual Prevalence for New Jersey High School Students
(percentage using in the past year)

Drug	1980	1986	1989
Alcohol	87.6	82.9	76.5
Marijuana	51.8	40.0	23.9
Hallucinogens	12.3	10.4	6.6
Cocaine	16.6	19.2	9.4

SOURCE: Fisher (1990).

According to the students, the perceived availability of marijuana is down, but the availability of cocaine and hallucinogens is up (see Table 3.3).

The factors that an increasing percentage of youth claim have prevented their own substance use are fear of physical harm, fear of trouble with the law, parental disapproval, and friends' disapproval. The same pattern exists for alcohol.

The perceived risk of occasional or regular use of marijuana has increased considerably (see Table 3.4), as has the perceived risk of having one or two drinks

Table 3.3

Perception of Drug Availability
for New Jersey High School Students
(percentage saying substance would be easy to obtain)

Drug	1980	1986	1989
Alcohol	93.9	88.8	91.4
Marijuana	89.8	82.8	79.9
Hallucinogens	47.3	50.0	54.4
Cocaine	47.4	58.0	59.9

SOURCE: Fisher (1990).

Table 3.4

**Perceived Health and Social Risks Resulting from
Marijuana Use for New Jersey High School Students
(percentage of respondents)**

	1980	1986	1989
Great	10.7	25.6	33.0
Slight or none	46.2	35.8	20.5

daily (see Table 3.5), although this increase in perceived risk has not resulted in a commensurate decline in alcohol use.[4]

Further analyses of the data show no substantial differences by area of the state or by socioeconomic status of the school. This finding is consistent with other surveys of youth, which generally have found little or no association between social class, or race, and drug use. However, some studies have shown higher rates of drug use among youth living in urban areas, as opposed to rural areas, and greater involvement in selling among those from poorer families (Elliott, Huizinga, and Menard, 1989).

Drug Abuse Warning Network: Emergency Room Episodes

Comparison of Trends in Newark and Other Cities

As shown in Figures 3.1 and 3.2, for most of the period from January 1989 through September 1990, Newark consistently exceeded Chicago, New York, Los Angeles, and Washington, D.C., in its rate of DAWN emergency room episodes per 100,000 residents.[5] For heroin, during the third quarter of 1989 and the

Table 3.5

**Perceived Risk Resulting from 1 or 2 Drinks Daily
for New Jersey High School Students
(percentage of respondents)**

	1980	1986	1989
Great	14.9	33.8	42.0
Slight or none	39.2	19.2	18.0

---

[4]This pattern is consistent with the findings of an experimental substance-abuse prevention program designed and evaluated by RAND (Ellickson and Bell, 1990).

[5]These figures include all episodes in the metropolitan area covered by DAWN, not just the municipality named. They are also based on weighted data from the redesigned DAWN sample and are not comparable with the data presented later in this section for the city of Newark and the target neighborhood.

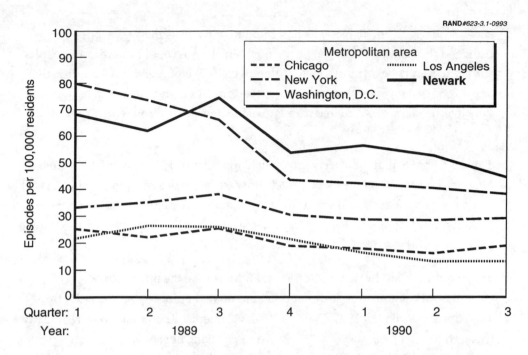

Figure 3.1—DAWN Cocaine-Related Emergency Room Episodes for Five Cities

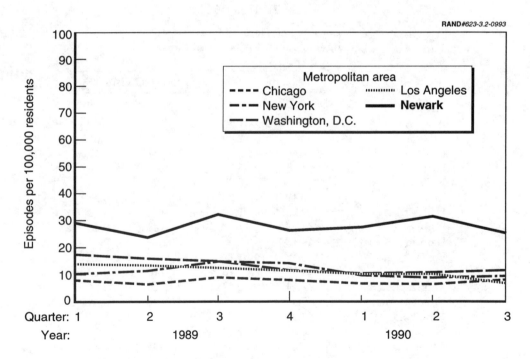

Figure 3.2—DAWN Heroin-Related Emergency Room Episodes for Five Cities

second quarter of 1990, Newark had more than twice as many episodes per hundred thousand population as the next highest metropolitan area. Per capita differences may be attributable to different rates of emergency room utilization across cities. However, Newark still exceeds most other cities when cocaine and heroin episodes are calculated as a rate of all emergency room episodes for all causes.

Table 3.6 shows that Newark was consistently high in 1989 and 1990. In 1990, Newark had the highest rate per 1,000 emergency room visits among all DAWN cities for cocaine and the second highest for heroin. Unlike most other cities shown on the table, cocaine and heroin episodes per 1,000 emergency room visits in Newark did not decline between 1989 and 1990.

These figures also show that the Newark PMSA, like the others shown, experienced a significant decline in cocaine-related episodes between the third and fourth quarters of 1989 and that the level of episodes remained fairly steady through the third quarter of 1990. More recent data, not shown, indicate renewed upward trends in Newark and most other metropolitan areas. In

Table 3.6

**DAWN Cocaine and Heroin Mentions per 1,000
Emergency Room Visits for All Causes**

Metropolitan	Number of Mentions per 1,000 Visits			
	Cocaine		Heroin or Morphine	
Area	1989	1990	1989	1990
Atlanta	4.17	2.60	0.09	0.07
Baltimore	2.48	3.90	1.47	2.18
Boston	1.85	1.20	0.82	0.56
Buffalo	1.36	0.85	0.20	0.32
Chicago	3.49	2.28	1.08	0.95
Dallas	2.26	1.40	0.51	0.48
Denver	1.92	1.30	0.44	0.40
Detroit	4.13	2.50	1.19	0.99
Los Angeles	3.56	1.77	1.76	1.03
Miami	1.97	1.40	0.10	0.10
Minneapolis	1.14	0.49	0.20	0.14
New Orleans	7.35	4.52	0.74	0.34
New York	4.21	3.73	1.75	1.12
Newark	**6.59**	**7.40**	**2.73**	**4.06**
Philadelphia	6.41	4.80	1.35	1.42
Phoenix	1.92	1.13	0.91	0.65
St. Louis	2.34	0.89	0.33	0.13
San Diego	1.07	1.22	0.88	1.27
San Francisco	5.28	4.15	6.32	7.15
Seattle	3.04	1.29	1.60	1.02
Washington D.C.	7.50	4.30	2.11	1.20

Newark and the other cities, the level of heroin-related episodes remained rather constant throughout the period shown. Judging from these data, Newark's heroin problem clearly exceeds that of the other cities. In Newark, heroin represents 14 percent of all drugs mentioned in DAWN episodes. Next to San Francisco, at 21 percent for heroin, this is the highest rate among all DAWN sites. Again, data for more-recent quarters show increases in the number of heroin mentions, with Newark showing some of the highest increases.

DAWN Episodes in Newark

The figures in the preceding section show the DAWN indicators of drug abuse turning down, in the second half of 1989, in most major metropolitan areas throughout the U. S. In particular, the number of DAWN cocaine-related episodes decreased by about 14 percent between 1988 and 1989 nationwide.

Raw counts of emergency room drug episodes for the broader Newark metropolitan area between the first quarter of 1987 and the last quarter of 1989, shown in Figure 3.3, are consistent with the national trend in that they show a leveling-off of episodes between 1988 and 1989 and, with the exception of the

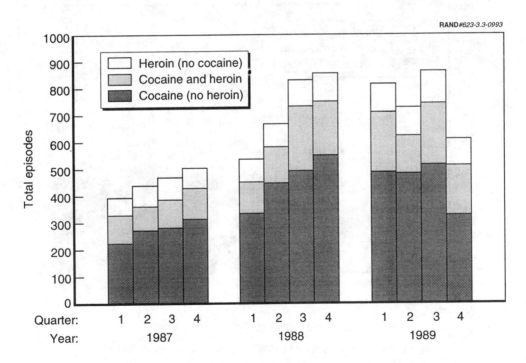

Figure 3.3—Newark PMSA DAWN Emergency Room Episodes

32

third quarter, a declining number of episodes during 1989.[6] Cocaine and heroin are divided into three sections on the bars shown in this figure—cocaine episodes not involving heroin; cocaine episodes also involving heroin (known locally as "speed balling" when injected in combination); and heroin episodes not involving cocaine. It is easy to see that what had been a pattern of steady increases during 1987 and 1988 began to change in 1989. In addition, cocaine episodes that did not involve heroin stabilized and then declined sharply at the end of the year. Heroin episodes that did not include cocaine remained about the same throughout the whole period, with some increase in 1988 and again in the third quarter of 1989. Episodes involving both drugs increased dramatically in the summer of 1988 and have remained roughly at the same level since then. However, when we look at emergency room episodes in the same hospitals, involving only residents of the city of Newark, as shown in Figure 3.4, we see several differences. First, while the PMSA totals declined by 40 percent between the fourth quarter of 1988 and the fourth quarter of 1989, the number of episodes involving residents of the city increased by 11 percent. In the PMSA, episodes of cocaine without heroin accounted for well over half the total cases in most time

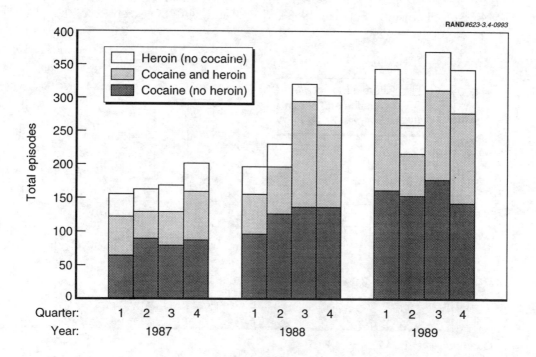

Figure 3.4—Newark City DAWN Emergency Room Episodes

___

[6]Data shown in the remaining figures in this section are based on raw counts of episodes in Newark hospitals for a consistently reporting panel of hospitals over the period January 1987 to December 1989.

periods; among the Newark residents, cocaine without heroin was more often about 45 percent of the total, with heroin (usually in combination with cocaine) involved in the majority of episodes.

Figure 3.4 also shows that most of the increase in emergency room cases among Newark residents in 1989 was associated with heroin episodes that did not involve cocaine, which were 50 percent higher in the last quarter of 1989 compared to a year earlier. The major increase in episodes involving heroin and cocaine in combination came in the second half of 1988, and the level has remained constant since then. The decline in these episodes during the second quarter of 1989 was due primarily to a decrease in the number of episodes at one facility during May, where the total number of emergency room visits also declined sharply for the month.

Reports of the CEWG for Newark also focused on the increasing use of heroin. The June 1990 report stated that heroin prevalence in Newark appeared to be rising. It suggested that the upturn might be "due to continued high purity and availability."[7] The December 1990 report noted a continued steady climb in the number of DAWN emergency room mentions of heroin and again attributed this to the high purity—about 50 percent on the street. It reported that "Snorting, rather than injection, is the most popular form of ingestion among younger users; it has also grown more common among older, chronic users trying to reduce their risk of being infected by human immunodeficiency virus (HIV)."[8] The June 1991 report stated that "Snorting continues to be common, particularly among young drug users."[9] This report also indicated that current street prices in Newark were about $15 per bag containing 25 to 35 milligrams.[10]

Episodes from the Target Neighborhood

In comparing the caseload from the three zip codes that include the target neighborhood with the caseload from elsewhere in the city (Figures 3.5 and 3.6),

---

[7]French (1990).

[8]French (1991a).

[9] French (1991b).

[10]A story in the *Los Angeles Times* (June 19, 1991, p. A5) presented evidence from a number of sources regarding the resurgence in heroin use. Besides pointing out that supplies of heroin were up (worldwide production has quadrupled since 1985), purity was up, and prices were low. The two experts who were quoted pointed out that every stimulant epidemic has been followed by an increased use of sedatives. They asserted that "Stimulants such as cocaine wear people out. As a result they often turn to sedatives like heroin to calm their nerves and to achieve a more soothing high." DEA figures show that street prices for southeast Asian heroin have dropped as low as 62 cents a milligram in Los Angeles and purity levels have soared above 18 percent, compared to purity levels around 4 percent in the early 1980s. The higher purity level allows the drug to be smoked or snorted, rather than requiring the more dangerous injection by needle.

34

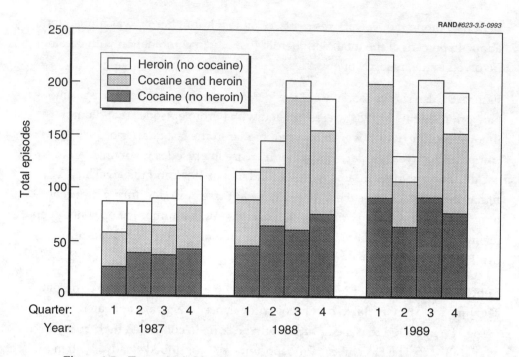

Figure 3.5—Target Neighborhood DAWN Emergency Room Episodes

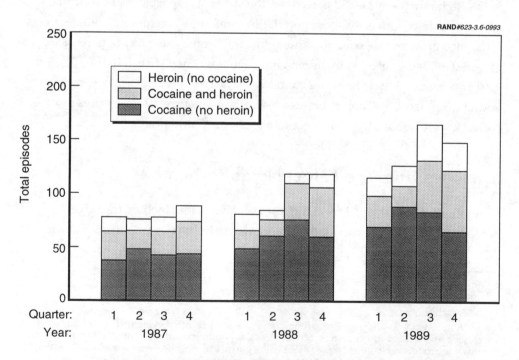

Figure 3.6—City of Newark Without the Target Neighborhood DAWN
Emergency Room Episodes

we see that total emergency room episodes involving heroin and/or cocaine decreased somewhat during 1989 for the target neighborhood but continued to increase for the rest of the city. The number of episodes involving cocaine and heroin in combination increased during the second half of 1989 in all of the city except the target neighborhood. In contrast, the decline in total emergency room episodes from the target neighborhood in 1989 is due largely to a decrease in the number of episodes involving heroin and cocaine in combination.

In 1987, episodes from the target neighborhood accounted for about half of the total for the city (despite the fact that the population of the three zip codes that produce these episodes is only about 26 percent of the city's total). In 1988 the target neighborhood produced almost two-thirds of the total episodes, and then in 1989 the proportion decreased to about half again. Given the higher per capita rate of emergency room episodes and higher rate of heroin-involved episodes, it might appear that the target neighborhood is more intensely involved with drug abuse than the rest of the city. If all of the episodes involved different individuals, the rate in the last quarter of 1989 for the target neighborhood would be one in 75 persons. However, the neighborhood probably has a high rate of intravenous (IV) drug users with AIDS and other chronic conditions who would be expected to repeatedly visit emergency rooms for primary AIDS care and/or chronic effects of drug abuse. It is also possible that target neighborhood residents have greater access to emergency rooms and/or that other locations in the city offer greater alternative sources of medical care for substance abuse problems. We cannot assume a direct relationship between DAWN and the prevalence of drug abuse.

Because we do not have patients' zip codes in our 1990 data, it is not possible to report on later trends in the target neighborhood versus the rest of the city.

Emergency Room Caseload Characteristics

While the DAWN data we have are now somewhat dated, they remain helpful in arriving at a better understanding of the characteristics of emergency room caseloads related to drug abuse and how they vary in the city.

The data show no differences in the disposition of emergency room episodes based on patient zip codes. Rather, throughout the city, 50 percent of all patients are admitted as inpatients, either for continued care or for observation overnight; 40 percent are treated and released from the emergency room (sometimes with referral for further treatment); and almost 10 percent are coded as having left the emergency room against medical advice.

36

Figure 3.7 shows differences in age and gender between DAWN patients from the NFB target neighborhood and the rest of the city for emergency room episodes involving cocaine but not heroin. The most important difference is the greater representation of females from the target neighborhood. In the target neighborhood, females account for 50 percent of the cocaine emergency room episodes among persons in their twenties. In the rest of the city, females represent only about 35 percent of this total. In the older age group, 30 and over, females are about 30 percent of the total in both the target neighborhood and elsewhere in the city. The numbers for heroin, and for heroin and cocaine in combination, are too small for the differences we see to be statistically significant. But for the cocaine-only cases, the difference between the target neighborhood and the rest of the city in the 20- to 29-year-old age group, after controlling for the number of females in the two areas, is statistically significant.[11] This difference is especially interesting, because, if we look at the age group 19 and under, we see that the target neighborhood females account for only 10 percent

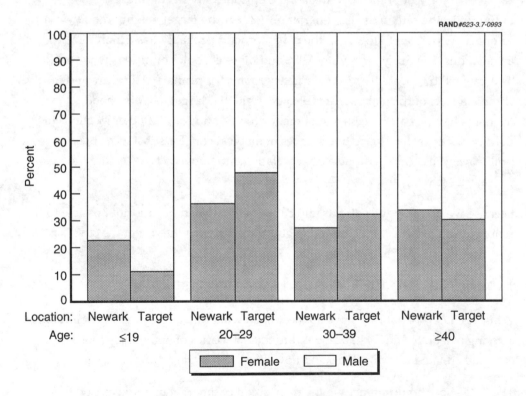

Figure 3.7—Age and Gender Comparisons Between City Total and the Target Neighborhood Among Cocaine-Only Episodes

_____

[11]Chi-Square 11.057 with a p-value of 0.001.

of the episodes, while elsewhere in the city they account for 25 percent of all episodes in this age group. This seems to suggest that the heavy involvement of females in the target neighborhood doesn't begin until the young-adult years.

For cocaine cases, there is no major difference in age distribution between the two areas; but for heroin, target neighborhood residents in the emergency rooms are older than are residents from elsewhere in the city. Male heroin cases differ significantly in their age distribution. Over one-third of the men from the target neighborhood are over 40 years old, and 88 percent are over 30,[12] whereas in the rest of the city only 20 percent are over 40 years old and almost 30 percent are under 30.

The older male heroin users are likely to be long-term addicts in need of increasing medical attention and are less likely to be working or involved with families. These users may also help explain the disproportionately large number of emergency room episodes from the NFB target neighborhood. The difference in age distribution between the target neighborhood and the rest of the city suggests that the former is attracting (or retaining) more than its share of these older addicts, possibly because of the large number of shelter and treatment programs located in the neighborhood or because drug connections are more plentiful there.

Drug-Related Deaths Reported by Medical Examiners

Medical examiners from each of the Newark PMSA counties—Essex, Morris, Sussex, and Union—participate in the DAWN system. Although the DAWN data-collection forms provide for the coding of zip codes of decedents, this information was missing for all Newark PMSA cases for the years 1987 through 1989.[13] Therefore our discussion of drug-related deaths is based on data from the entire metropolitan area, which, as we saw in the preceding section, has shown considerably different recent trends from those of the city of Newark.

DAWN data for the Newark metropolitan area indicate that the number of deaths related to drug use began to decline in 1989, with a total of 177 deaths that year from all drugs, down 19 percent from 1988 and 40 percent from 1987.[14]

---

[12]The older age lends further credence to the earlier suggestion that the larger number of episodes per capita in the target neighborhood may be due to repeat visits, rather than more drug abusers.

[13]We were unable to obtain complete data for 1990 from the National Institute on Drug Abuse.

[14]These deaths do not include cases in which AIDS was reported or where homicide was the cause of death. The majority of AIDS cases in Newark involve intravenous drug users, and over the past few years 60 to 70 deaths were coded as homicides of drug abusers.

Forty-seven percent of deaths reported in DAWN involved the use of alcohol in addition to drugs.

The number of drug abuse deaths as a percentage of all deaths reported by medical examiners has remained at 3.7 percent over the past few years, down from about 6.8 percent in 1987. The Newark PMSA compares well with several eastern neighbors, such as New York, Philadelphia, Boston, and Washington, D.C., where drug-related deaths represent a higher percentage of total deaths. However, compared with metropolitan areas of comparable size around the country, the rate of drug-related deaths in Newark is higher. Table 3.7 shows drug-related deaths for Newark and a number of other DAWN sites.

DAWN reports the number of times selected drugs are mentioned per 1000 medical examiner–reported deaths from all causes. In 1987, Newark had the second highest rate of cocaine mentions and the third highest rate of heroin mentions among all DAWN sites. By 1989 this standing had shifted somewhat; Newark's cocaine rate was down to fourth highest in the nation, and its heroin rate had slipped to 14th highest.

Drug Use Characteristics of Decedents

Multiple drugs (or a single drug used in combination with alcohol) were present in 75 percent of the deaths. Cocaine was involved in over 80 percent of the 1989

Table 3.7

Drug-Related Deaths Reported by Medical Examiners

Metropolitan Area	1989 DAWN Drug-Related Deaths[a] per 100,000 Population	Percentage of All Medical Examiner– Reported Deaths[a]
New York	21.0	7.3
Philadelphia	12.2	6.3
San Diego	11.4	9.7
Washington, D.C.	9.9	11.8
Newark	**9.4**	**3.7**
Boston	9.0	7.4
Dallas	6.8	4.1
Phoenix	6.0	4.1
Miami	5.8	2.8
Denver	4.2	0.9
Cleveland	3.4	2.1
Minneapolis	2.2	1.5

SOURCE: DAWN Report, 1989.

[a]Different areas have different regulations regarding the requirement to report deaths to medical examiners. These differences affect comparisons across metropolitan areas.

cases in the Newark PMSA. Twenty percent of the decedents had used cocaine and heroin in combination. Only 7 percent involved heroin without cocaine. However, the DAWN exclusion of deaths due to AIDS deflates the number of deaths related to heroin use.

The number of nonhomicide deaths involving heroin decreased steadily from 107 in 1987 to 49 in 1989, in spite of the fact that usage rates increased dramatically.[15] While heroin deaths were declining, the number of deaths involving cocaine use increased significantly between 1987 and 1988. However, by 1989 cocaine deaths, too, began to decline, moving down from 177 in 1988 to 147 in 1989. Over this three-year period, the number of deaths involving heroin and cocaine in combination also declined. Three-year totals for all DAWN deaths and the number of mentions of each drug type—cocaine, heroin, cocaine and heroin in combination, and other drugs—are presented in Table 3.8.

Demographics of Decedents

Most decedents in 1989, as in previous years, were black, male, and over 30 years old. Females, whites, and Hispanics seemed to be decreasing as a percentage of the total over the three years from 1987 through 1989. Only six youths under 18 were involved in (nonhomicide) drug-related deaths during the year, and 19 to 29 year olds accounted for about 25 percent of the total. Those over age 35 increased from 41 percent in 1987 to 45 percent in 1989. Table 3.9 shows the age, race or ethnicity, and gender breakdowns for the Newark PMSA.

Table 3.8

**Frequency of Drugs Mentioned in Drug-Involved
Medical Examiner–Reported Deaths**

Drug Mentions	1987	1988	1989
Total medical examiner–reported drug deaths	246	206	174
All cocaine	158	177	147
All heroin/morphine	107	77	49
% in combination with cocaine	63	84	75
Alcohol in combination	85	81	85
All other drugs	234	171	131

SOURCE: DAWN Reports 1987–1989.

---

[15]While the total drug deaths declined during this period in several other metropolitan areas as well, most saw an increase in the percentage of heroin deaths. Several changes in DAWN tabulation and reporting practices could be affecting the numbers during this period. We need 1990 data to determine whether the trend suggested here continued.

Table 3.9

Demographics of DAWN Medical Examiner Cases 1987–1989

	1987		1988		1989	
	#	%	#	%	#	%
Age						
18 & under	3	1.2	6	2.9	3	1.7
19–24	31	12.6	32	15.5	20	12.9
25–29	41	16.7	39	18.9	24	13.5
30–34	70	28.4	42	20.3	47	26.4
35+	101	41.0	87	42.2	80	44.9
Race or ethnicity						
Black	129	52.4	123	59.7	106	61.2
White	95	38.6	71	34.5	57	32.6
Hispanic	22	8.9	12	5.8	10	5.6
Sex						
Male	183	74.4	162	78.6	143	81.5
Female	63	25.6	44	21.3	31	18.5

SOURCE: DAWN data for the Newark PMSA.

As noted above, most drug-related deaths in the Newark area in recent years have involved the use of cocaine. The cause of death reported in cases involving cocaine is usually accidental—as opposed to suicide or homicide, the other major causes of drug-involved deaths. The demographics of decedents who had used cocaine changed very little from 1987 to 1989.

The decedents who used heroin and cocaine in combination shared some of the characteristics of those who used heroin. For example, they tended to be older, and males represented a very large percentage of the total deaths. However, like the cocaine users, they were predominantly black, while the majority of decedents who used heroin without cocaine were white.

Deaths from drugs other than cocaine or heroin were more often caused by suicide (33 percent). The decedents were younger and more often female and white compared to other medical examiner–reported deaths. The least frequent cause of death was the use of alcohol in combination with other drugs.

The characteristics of drug-related homicides are somewhat different from those of other drug-related deaths. Not surprisingly, these involve younger decedents—5 percent were 18 and under, 35 percent were under 25. Only about 20 percent were over 35 years old, compared to over 40 percent for drug-related deaths in general. A larger percentage of this group (86 percent) were black. Hispanics were 10 percent of homicide drug cases, compared to 6 percent of nonhomicide cases. Females were a lower percentage of homicide drug cases than of nonhomicide cases. The drug most often involved was cocaine. Heroin,

heroin and cocaine in combination, and other drugs were involved in fewer homicide cases than nonhomicide cases.

Arrests for Drug Possession and Sales in Newark

The DAWN emergency room data point to a substantial increase in drug-related emergency room episodes between the first quarter of 1987 and the last quarter of 1989, as well as an increasing proportion of cases involving heroin. Examining arrest data from the NPD, we see similar and continued upward trends.

Adults. In 1990, the NPD arrested 5,268 adults for drug violations—2,824 for sales and 2,444 for possession. Data from the NPD Narcotics Bureau database show that arrests for drug *possession* in the city increased by almost 24 percent between the second half of 1989 and the second half of 1990, as shown in Figure 3.8. The percentage of arrests involving cocaine decreased slightly from 59 to 56 percent, while that involving heroin increased from 12.5 to 20.7 percent. Within the target neighborhood, the increase in total drug possession arrests was slightly lower (33 percent), as shown in Figure 3.9, but heroin arrests increased by more than 300 percent.

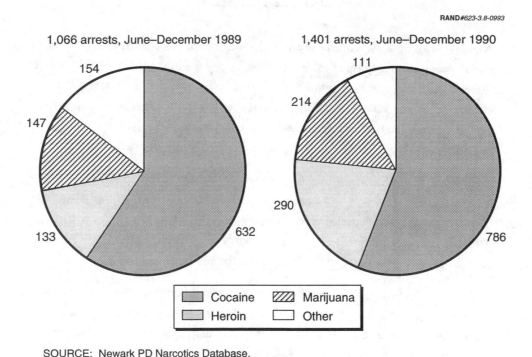

RAND#623-3.8-0993

1,066 arrests, June–December 1989   1,401 arrests, June–December 1990

SOURCE: Newark PD Narcotics Database.

Figure 3.8—Arrests for Drug Possession by Type of Drug: City of Newark (except airport)

RAND#623-3.9-0993

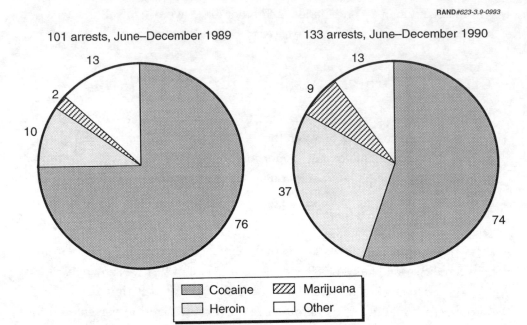

101 arrests, June–December 1989   133 arrests, June–December 1990

| Cocaine | Marijuana |
| Heroin | Other |

SOURCE: Newark PD Narcotics Database.

Figure 3.9—Arrests for Drug Possession by Type of Drug: Newark Fighting Back Target Neighborhood

Arrests for drug *sales* within the city held about constant over this period, with more than half involving cocaine. The major change in the mix of drugs was the increase in the percentage involving heroin, up from 15.5 to 25.5 percent, as shown in Figure 3.10. The number of sales arrests in the target neighborhood also remained fairly stable, but the shift toward heroin was even more pronounced—up from 17.8 to 36.4 percent, as shown in Figure 3.11.

Aggregate arrest data for the entire year of 1990 show that drug arrests accounted for 22 percent of all adult arrests (and 18 percent of all female arrests) in Newark in 1990. Females were somewhat more likely than males to be arrested for sales rather than possession, with 63 percent of their arrests being for sales versus 52 percent of males being arrested for sales.

The most interesting difference between males and females is their different age distribution. Table 3.10 shows arrests by gender, age, and race or ethnicity. For males the peak age of arrest is 18, after which the numbers arrested decline in each age group. For females there is also a peak at age 18; but after a temporary decline, the numbers increase again among females in their early twenties, reaching another peak at age 24. Table 3.11 shows the percentage of males and females arrested in each age group.

Table 3.10

Adults Arrested for Drug Violations by the Newark Police Department in 1990

| Offense | | Ages | | | | | | | | | | | | | Race and Ethnic Origin | | | | | |
		18	19	20	21	22	23	24	25–29	30–34	35–39	40–44	45+	Total	White	Black	Asia Pacific	Hisp.	Non-Hisp.	Total
Narcotics drug laws	Male	424	405	392	298	286	271	221	994	614	346	201	156	4,608						
	Female	31	23	22	33	37	37	42	173	134	76	29	23	660						
	Total	455	428	414	331	323	308	263	1167	748	422	230	179	5,268	861	4,403	4	668	4,596	5,268
Narcotics sales/mfg.	Male	250	241	205	171	150	156	116	503	291	154	92	80	2,409						
	Female	19	17	20	24	23	26	23	114	70	43	20	16	415						
	Total	269	258	225	195	173	182	139	617	361	197	112	96	2,824	472	2,352		418	2,406	2,824
Narcotics possession	Male	174	164	187	127	136	115	105	491	323	192	109	76	2,199						
	Female	12	6	2	9	14	11	19	59	64	33	9	7	245						
	Total	186	170	189	136	150	126	124	550	387	225	118	83	2,444	389	2,051	4	250	2,190	2,444

SOURCE: Newark Police Department.

44

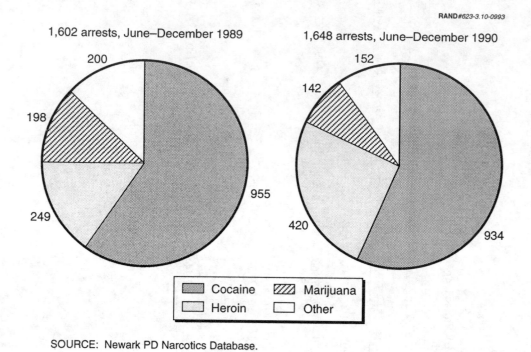

1,602 arrests, June–December 1989   1,648 arrests, June–December 1990

Cocaine	▨	Marijuana
Heroin	☐	Other

SOURCE: Newark PD Narcotics Database.

**Figure 3.10—Arrests for Drug Sales by Type of Drug: City of Newark
(except airport)**

For both sales and possession arrests, the percentage of males under 20 is double that of females. While 50 percent of the males arrested are under age 25, only 34 percent of the females are in this younger group. However, the percentage of females arrested in their late twenties and thirties is higher than that of males in the same age group.

While the number of females arrested in each age group is quite small and more subject to variability, we do see the same pattern for sales and possession in 1989 and 1990. The differences may be due to different motivations for drug dealing among males and females. Perhaps as they become older, men begin to recruit women with whom they are involved to work for them and/or obtain drugs for them (as reported by one of the dealers we interviewed). Or perhaps the differences in age distribution are due to differences in law enforcement practices. Police may be less suspicious of younger females than of younger males.

The figures in Table 3.11 are consistent with the reports of the drug dealers we interviewed (mostly male) who reported that, like themselves, most dealers were young. Also, since most of our informants were males, the table suggests that

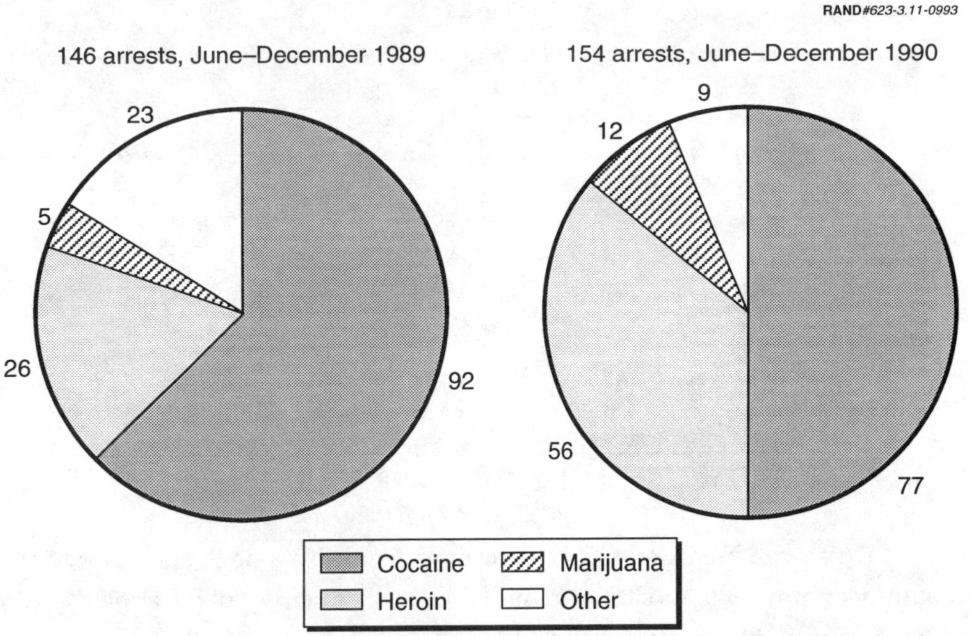
RAND#623-3.11-0993
146 arrests, June–December 1989
23
5
26
92
154 arrests, June–December 1990
9
12
56
77
Cocaine
Marijuana
Heroin
Other

SOURCE: Newark PD Narcotics Database.

Figure 3.11—Arrests for Drug Sales by Type of Drug: Target Neighborhood

more information is needed about the career paths of women involved in drugs and the criminal justice system, especially because of the relatively large number of female dealers we found in the target neighborhood.

Juveniles. During 1990, the NPD arrested 906 juveniles for narcotics violations. In contrast to the trend for adults, this number represents a decrease of 6 percent from the previous year. Possession arrests increased by 14 percent between 1989 and 1990, but sales arrests declined by 21 percent.

Ninety-four percent of the total arrested were males. Drug arrests accounted for 22 percent of all arrests of juveniles in Newark in 1990. Among drug arrests, 57 percent were for sales offenses, and most sales, 87 percent, involved substances in the combined category of opium, cocaine, morphine, heroin, and codeine. Very few sales arrests were for sale of marijuana. Among possession arrests, marijuana accounted for 20 percent of the total arrests, and the combined cocaine-heroin category accounted for 77 percent.

Table 3.11

Age Distribution of Male and Female Arrestees in 1990
(percent)

	All Narcotics Drug Laws		Narcotics Sales/Mfg.		Narcotics Possession	
	Male	Female	Male	Female	Male	Female
Under 20	18	8	20	9	15	7
20–24	32	26	33	28	30	22
25–29	22	26	21	27	22	24
30–34	13	20	12	17	15	26
35–39	8	12	6	10	9	13
40 +	8	8	7	9	8	6
Total	100	100	100	100	100	100

SOURCE: Newark Police Department.

Table 3.12 shows a breakdown of juvenile drug arrests by gender, age, and racial or ethnic composition. As shown in this table, only 14 percent of the adolescents arrested were in the preadolescent or early adolescent ages (even though they account for 62 percent of the juvenile population over age nine). Not surprisingly, the arrest rate greatly increases with age for males. By age 15, assuming each arrest in 1990 involved a different individual, one in 17 males was arrested during the year (per the 1990 census). For 17-year-old males, the chances of being arrested in 1990 were one in six. Females, while representing fewer arrests, were more likely to be arrested for sales than for possession and were less likely to be arrested under age 16.

The Substance Abuse Treatment Population

The DAWN emergency room, medical examiner, and arrest data provide a picture of who is being harmed by drugs. Data on participants in treatment programs show who is trying to get help. The Division of Alcoholism and Drug Abuse, New Jersey Department of Health, maintains a statewide episode-based data system on drug treatment center admissions. Data are submitted by individual treatment centers to the state. The database contains information on demographic and social characteristics of treatment clientele, their drug use history, and drug use characteristics at admission. The information in this subsection, which comes from this system, describes Essex County residents

Table 3.12

Juveniles Arrested for Drug Violations by the Newark Police Department in 1990

Offense	Ages							Race and Ethnic Origin			
	Under 10	10–12	13–14	15	16	17	Total Under 18	White	Black	Hisp.	Non-Hisp.
All narcotics drug laws											
Male	2	6	112	135	220	373	848				
Female	1	1	2	8	20	27	58				
Total	3	6	114	143	240	400	906	97	809	87	819
Narcotics sales/mfg.											
Male	1	4	68	80	125	201	479				
Female	1	1	1	3	14	20	39				
Total	2	4	69	83	139	221	518	47	471	42	476
Narcotics possession											
Male	1	2	44	55	95	172	369				
Female			1	5	6	7	19				
Total	1	2	45	60	101	179	388	50	338	45	343

SOURCE: Newark Police Department.

admitted to treatment between January and June of 1990.[16] The majority of Essex County admissions are from Newark and are in treatment centers located in Newark.[17]

Table 3.13, from the December 1990 CEWG report for Newark, shows the primary, secondary, and tertiary drugs of abuse among treatment admissions from Essex County during the first half of 1990. A total of 73 percent abused heroin. Fifty-nine percent abused cocaine, which was most frequently reported as a secondary drug of abuse among heroin admissions. Cocaine appears as the primary drug of abuse in only 19 percent of the cases, but this is largely due to the treatment system's emphasis on methadone maintenance as a treatment modality. Alcohol and marijuana were both drugs of abuse in about 18 percent of all admissions, but, like cocaine, these drugs were reported as secondary and tertiary problems. The primary conclusion that can be drawn from these figures is that cocaine users are underrepresented in treatment compared to their representation in DAWN emergency room episodes and in arrests.

The characteristics of those who were admitted for cocaine and heroin as the primary drug of abuse and the method they used to administer the drug are shown in Tables 3.14 and 3.15. Thirty-eight percent of cocaine admissions and 36 percent of heroin admissions were female (slightly higher than the rate among emergency room cases). Among cocaine admissions, 75 percent were black, 15 percent Hispanic, and 10 percent white.

Most women reported smoking cocaine, while the predominant method of administration for men was snorting. Seven percent of cocaine admissions reported IV drug use, while 65 percent of heroin cases were IV users. According to the CEWG report, the rate of IV use is down, because the availability of higher-purity heroin and fear of AIDS have made snorting heroin an attractive alternative method of administration. However, although younger users tend to snort the drug, older users are still mostly IV users.

Cocaine admissions, like cocaine DAWN cases, were younger than heroin admissions. Almost 20 percent were 21 or younger. Only 30 percent were over

---

[16]It is important to note that this information describes only the treatment population, not the population of drug abusers in need of treatment. The characteristics of those in treatment reflect the availability of treatment services in the community. For example, methadone maintenance facilities can serve larger populations than residential rehabilitation facilities. The former serve heroin users exclusively and thus, by virtue of their existence, drive up the number of heroin treatment admissions.

[17]J. Farrell, New Jersey Division of Alcoholism and Drug Abuse; presentation to Fighting Back Substance Abuse Committee, February 4, 1991.

Table 3.13

Primary, Secondary, and Tertiary Drugs of Abuse by Residents of Essex County Admitted to Treatment Between January and June 1990

Drug	Primary	%	Secondary	%	Tertiary	%	Total[a]	%
Heroin	1,596	70.7	40	1.8	18	0.8	1.654	73.3
Cocaine	421	18.6	867	38.4	35	1.6	1.323	58.6
Other opiates	24	1.1	69	3.1	33	1.5	126	5.6
Alcohol	79	3.5	185	8.2	163	7.2	427	18.9
Marijuana	90	4.0	185	8.2	135	6.0	410	18.2
Hypnotics	22	1.0	26	1.2	32	1.4	80	3.5
Amphetamines	1	0.0	1	0.0	2	0.1	4	0.1
Others	25	1.1	28	1.2	24	1.1	77	3.4
No problem	0	0.0	857	37.9	1,816	80.4		
Total	2,258	100.0	2,258	100.0	2,258	100.0		

SOURCE: New Jersey State Department of Health, June 1990.
[a]Represents multiple reporting.

Table 3.14

Characteristics of Cocaine Treatment Admissions by Method of Drug Administration, Essex County Admissions

Characteristic	Number	Percentage of Total	Method of Administration		
			Smoking (percent)	Snorting (percent)	IV (percent)
Gender					
Male	260	62	31	60	9
Female	160	38	59	37	4
Race/ethnicity					
White	43	10	26	72	2
Black	314	75	50	42	8
Hispanic	63	15	16	79	5
Age					
14–21	79	19	39	61	0
22–30	214	51	47	48	5
31–40	115	27	36	50	14
> 40	12	3	33	50	17
Education					
< HS	207	49	38	55	7
HS graduate	156	37	43	51	6
> HS	58	14	53	36	9
Prior treatment					
No	253	60	38	56	6
Yes	168	40	47	53	10
Arrested/2 years					
No	253	60	45	46	9
Yes	168	40	36	58	6
Health insurance					
None	267	63	36	56	8
Private	59	14	38	58	4
Public	95	23	60	32	8
Treatment modality					
Detox	26	6	62	23	15
Outpatient	318	76	39	55	6
Residential	75	18	49	41	10

SOURCE: New Jersey State Department of Health, June 1990.

30. As was true with the heroin cases, the older group reported higher rates of IV cocaine use than the younger groups. The availability of snortable heroin may be drawing younger users into heroin use. The CEWG report shows that, for the first time, the age of heroin admissions has begun to decline.

Almost half of those admitted to treatment for both cocaine and heroin had not completed high school. More than half reported that they had never been in treatment previously. Cocaine admissions were more likely to have been

Table 3.15

**Characteristics of Heroin Treatment Admissions by Method of
Drug Administration, Essex County Admissions**

			Method of Administration	
Characteristic	Number	Column (percent)	Snorting (percent)	IV (percent)
Gender				
Male	1,026	64	26	74
Female	570	36	50	50
Race/ethnicity				
White	133	8	21	79
Black	1,162	73	35	65
Hispanic	298	19	39	61
Age				
14–21	73	5	82	18
22–30	443	28	54	46
31–40	801	50	27	73
> 40	276	17	13	87
Education				
< HS	713	45	33	67
HS graduate	633	40	36	64
> HS	250	16	35	65
Prior treatment				
No	886	56	37	66
Yes	710	44	32	62
Arrested/2 years				
No	1,265	79	34	63
Yes	331	21	38	68
Health insurance				
None	1,165	73	27	73
Private	66	4	43	57
Public	365	23	56	44
Treatment modality				
Detox	956	60	38	62
Maintenance	444	28	16	84
Outpatient	165	10	55	45
Residential	31	2	68	32

SOURCE: New Jersey State Department of Health, June 1990.

arrested, especially since criminal justice system diversions to treatment have been increasing.

In addition to the above data, we obtained some information about the clientele of treatment centers in Newark from Integrity Inc. This treatment center shared with us the same information it provides to the state system. The center's substance abuse treatment services include both residential and outpatient programs.

The center's fiscal 1989 and 1991 data show that the method of drug administration by their clients changed over time: Inhalation went up from 22.5 percent to 30 percent; smoking increased from 28 percent to 33 percent; IV use went down from 24 percent to 18 percent; and oral ingestion stayed about the same. This information lends support to the CEWG contention that the purity of street drugs and the fear of contracting AIDS have decreased the number of IV users and increased inhalation and smoking as methods of administration.

With regard to source of referral to treatment, the data show that referrals from agencies, friends, and family went down slightly from approximately 4 percent to 2 percent. Referrals from the criminal justice system, including the probation and parole segments, went up from 56 percent to 63 percent; self-referrals remained about the same at 25 percent.

The Integrity Inc. database also contained information on place of residence. Table 3.16 shows the number of patients and the percentage of total patients from the zip codes that include the NFB target neighborhood compared to the number and percentage of admissions from the rest of Newark. While admissions from the rest of the city increased by 18 percent, admissions from the target neighborhood increased by 39 percent over the three-year period. Patients from zips in the target area now make up more than half of the Newark caseload at Integrity Inc. Because Integrity House is located on the boundary of the target neighborhood, it may be very well known to residents of the area, and this may explain the large percentage of admissions from the neighborhood. Nonetheless, the fact remains that participation by residents of the neighborhood in the treatment programs of Integrity House has increased substantially between 1989 and 1991.

Table 3.16

Integrity Inc. Newark Caseload by Zip Code of Patient

Zip Code	FY 89 No.	FY 89 %	FY 90 No.	FY 90 %	FY 91 No.	FY 91 %	1989–1991 % change
07102	38	15.5	32	10.7	39	11.3	2.6
07103	30	12.2	49	16.4	75	21.7	60.0
07108	26	10.6	45	15.1	47	13.6	44.7
07114	20	8.2	20	6.7	25	7.2	20.0
Total	114	46.5	146	48.8	186	53.8	38.7
Other Newark	131	53.5	153	51.2	160	46.2	18.1
Total Newark caseload	245		299		346		29.1

SOURCE: Integrity Inc., Newark, NJ.

53

With similar data from other Newark treatment providers, the Fighting Back initiative could develop baseline data on target neighborhood residents in treatment and could monitor changes in light of future outreach efforts. Our other indicator data suggest that the zip codes in the NFB target area may contain the highest concentration of drug abusers in Newark.

Community Perceptions

A 1989 telephone survey of residents in Essex and West Hudson counties found that a large number of respondents believed that drugs were the most important problem facing their neighborhood (Chavis, Kopacsi, and Lazarus, 1989). Drugs were mentioned by 35 percent of the population, more than any other single problem. Among Newark residents, the percentage indicating drugs as the main problem was even higher. Thirty-nine percent of the Newark respondents volunteered that drugs were the most important problem facing their neighborhood.[18] When asked about specific community problems, 68 percent of those surveyed in Newark agreed that drug dealing was a major problem, about the same percentage found in other urban areas of the two counties. Only 23 percent of those from suburban areas of Essex and West Hudson counties agreed that drug dealing was a major problem.

During a tenant-organizing meeting in the NFB target neighborhood in early 1991, residents conducted a small survey of tenants in a HUD Section 8 apartment building. Among the residents surveyed, 88 percent indicated that drug abuse was a problem of the highest priority. Unemployment was the only problem given higher priority by these residents.

_____

[18]In a community survey of Los Angeles residents conducted about the same time, only 13 percent of the respondents indicated drugs when asked an open-ended question about what they thought was the worst thing about the Los Angeles area.

4. Community Resources for Substance Abuse Treatment and Prevention

Background

As part of this needs assessment, we inventoried existing substance abuse treatment resources in Newark to provide baseline information for a substance abuse treatment services clearinghouse that NFB was planning to establish. We attempted to identify all programs that served predominantly Newark residents, and then conducted a census of those programs to find out what populations they serve, their capacity and caseloads, their screening and eligibility procedures, their costs and program features, and their personnel.

In the following pages, we summarize what we learned from the providers surveyed, including information on available treatment capacity, the characteristics of existing programs, and the populations they serve. We also describe what we have identified from interviews with program providers as unmet needs for treatment in Newark and barriers to obtaining existing treatment services. Finally, we turn to an overview of school and community-based prevention programs.

Inventory Methods

In designing the treatment programs inventory, we used the existing categories of treatment modalities and environments as defined by the New Jersey Client-Oriented Data Acquisition Process (CODAP) because we expected Newark providers to be familiar with its terms and definitions.

At the time of our inventory in 1991, the New Jersey CODAP system defined five major kinds of treatment modalities and environments:

1. *Detoxification,* involving administration of medical help to short-term inpatients to end immediate drug use and overcome the pains and hazards of withdrawal

2. *Drug-free outpatient treatment*, involving a variety of counseling (group, one-to-one, family) and educational activities

3. *Methadone maintenance programs,* in which opiate users are supplied with regular doses of methadone that block the effects of a heroin high

4. *Residential rehabilitation programs*, in which residents are exposed to systematic and continuous efforts to help them face up to their addictive and dysfunctional lifestyles and adopt more functional forms of behavior

5. *Intensive day-care programs*, which share the features of residential rehabilitation programs, but clients return to their own homes at night.

Another type of program, often having only limited openings, is community aftercare or reentry programs. These programs offer follow-up services and continuing support to individuals who have completed rehabilitation programs.

Finally, a number of programs exist that offer collateral services, such as housing, job training, and child care to substance abusers in treatment and/or to their families.[1] Such programs were not separately inventoried in this study, but when collateral services are available through a treatment program, they have been included as program features rather than separate programs.

Different modalities can be delivered individually or combined in a series that begins with chemical detoxification, proceeds to residential rehabilitation, transitions to outpatient group counseling, and, finally, involves aftercare programs. There are other combinations and many customized programs exist in Newark. For example, one inpatient detoxification program with a duration of 5 to 6 days tries very hard to retain patients in the hospital for a longer period, about 21 days, for rehabilitation services. This is really more of a custom program than what we think of as normal detoxification, especially inpatient detoxification.

To select the population for the survey, we first identified 26 organizations in the Newark area from a variety of sources and directories of substance abuse treatment facilities.[2] We then sent letters to each of these organizations describing our survey and requesting their cooperation.[3] Finally, we conducted telephone interviews with the director (or designee) of each program offering substance abuse treatment associated with these organizations.

We have no guarantee that we have identified all such programs in the Newark area. Given resource constraints, the population had to be limited to programs that we had reason to believe served predominantly Newark residents. Outpatient programs in Essex County in municipalities outside Newark were thought to serve predominantly local residents rather than Newark residents.

---

[1]See partial list in Appendix A.
[2]Appendix B shows the sources we referred to.
[3]See Appendix C for a list of the organizations included in the survey.

However, major inpatient facilities, such as Turning Point and the East Orange General Hospital, were easily identified as facilities that, although they are not located in Newark, serve a large Newark patient population. Until a recent revision in data-collection procedures, the statewide data system for tracking treatment admissions (CODAP) did not capture the zip codes of patients and therefore could not report on admissions below the county of residence. Future efforts should be able to better identify the programs that serve Newark residents.

Of the 26 organizations on our original list, two were no longer in existence, and one was actually a program within another organization included on our list, rather than a separate provider. All of the remaining organizations we contacted cooperated enthusiastically with our survey, referring us to individual treatment program directors and facilitating the data-collection process. Information that they could not provide over the phone, many supplied by mail. In the next subsection, we describe the programs operated in 1991 by the organizations we surveyed.

Characteristics of Existing Programs

At the time of our inventory, the 23 organizations we surveyed administered 47 different treatment programs, as shown in Table 4.1. Some providers administered only one program, while others offered as many as seven.

Table 4.1

Treatment Programs in Newark

Treatment Modality/Environment	No. of Programs	Total Capacity	Comments
Methadone maintenance programs	2	930	
Inpatient detox programs	5	93	
(1 features a methadone component)			
(2 are outside the city of Newark)			
Outpatient detox programs	2	930	
(1 features a methadone component)			
Residential rehabilitation programs	13	624	Alcohol & drug
(7 are outside the city of Newark, but serve Newark residents)			
(2 for alcohol only)		65	Alcohol only
Intensive day-care rehabilitation programs	4	165	
(1 program is outside the city of Newark)			
Outpatient rehabilitation programs	15	3,331	Alcohol & drug
(2 for alcohol only)		70	Alcohol only
Reentry programs	6	398	

SOURCE: RAND inventory, 1991.

The most common type of program available to Newark residents was the drug-free rehabilitation program, about half of which were residential (total capacity approximately 700) and half outpatient (total capacity approximately 3,400). In addition, there were four intensive day programs for substance abuse rehabilitation (total capacity approximately 165). About 2 percent of the space was reserved for alcohol-only clients. There were also seven detoxification programs and two methadone maintenance programs (total capacity approximately 2,000) that primarily serve heroin users. The six aftercare/reentry programs in Newark had a combined capacity of about 400 clients.

Populations Served

Figure 4.1 shows the key population groups served by each existing program. For each modality or environment category, the matrix shows provider names, eligible age and gender groups served, and special populations within each (such as AIDS patients; criminal justice cases; Spanish speakers; and the pregnant, homeless, and mentally ill).

The overall capacity, as shown on Table 4.1, is misleading, because much of that capacity was available only to certain subgroups within the overall population in need of treatment. Figure 4.2 shows that 41 of the 47 treatment programs we inventoried were restricted to certain groups. The remaining six programs were available to males and females of all age groups without restriction.

Eight of the 41 programs shown in Figure 4.2 served male and female adolescents only. Three of these were restricted to adolescent males, and one to adolescent females. Another 16 programs were for adults only, plus two for adult males only and two for adult females. Two other programs served only criminal justice system referrals, and two served only Department of Corrections clientele. Four were strictly for veterans, four were limited to Spanish-speaking persons, and one served only the dually diagnosed mentally ill. In total, there were four culture-specific and eight gender-specific programs.

There is good news and bad news in program restriction policies. The good news is that they are designed specifically for the groups they serve and aim to be more sensitive to their needs. The bad news is that there are so few of them and that so few treatment modalities and environments are available per group. For example, for young females, specifically, one residential rehabilitation program was reported, serving about 10 girls, but there were no outpatient or intensive day-care rehabilitation programs for this group. (Of course, adolescent females can attend other programs available to all adolescents or to all age groups. See Figure 4.1.)

RAND#6623-4.1a-0993

Figure 4.1—Substance Abuse Treatment programs: Populations Served

Populations served matrix. Programs (rows) by population group. Columns are organized by age group (Adolescents, Adults, All ages), each divided into Male only, Female only, and Both, each with categories: Criminal, Homeless, Mentally ill, Pregnant, Spanish speaking, AIDS. A dot (●) indicates the population is served. Only the "Adults—Both" and "All ages—Both" columns contain entries; all Adolescent, Male only, and Female only columns are empty.

Program	Adults — Both						All ages — Both					
	AIDS	Criminal	Homeless	Mentally ill	Pregnant	Spanish speaking	AIDS	Criminal	Homeless	Mentally ill	Pregnant	Spanish speaking
Methadone maintenance												
18-1 Spectrum Health Care, Newark							●	●	●	●	●	●
23-3 VA Medical Center, Newark	●	●	●	●								
Inpatient detox												
02-1 Catholic Community Services, Newark[2]	●	●	●	●	●	●						
15-1 St. Michael's Hospital, Newark	●	●	●	●		●						
23-4 VA Medical Center, East Orange	●		●	●								
26-5 Straight & Narrow, Inc., Paterson							●	●	●	●	●	
27-1 East Orange General Hospital, East Orange	●	●	●	●	●							
Outpatient detox												
06-1 Essex Substance Abuse Treatment Center, Inc., Newark[3]	●	●	●	●	●	●						
18-2 Spectrum Health Care, Newark	●				●							
Rehab—outpatient												
02-2 Catholic Community Services, Newark							●	●	●	●	●	●
03-2 Choices, Inc., Newark[4]	●	●	●	●	●							
04-2 CURA, Inc., Newark	●	●	●		●	●						

SOURCE: RAND inventory, 1991.

[1] Some programs restrict minimum age to mid-adolescent or older
[2] Ages 17 and over
[3] Juveniles under special circumstances
[4] Substance abuser and family members (including children)
[5] Alcohol only

RAND#623-4.1b-0993

Figure 4.1—continued

Rehab—outpatient programs. Dots indicate services offered, organized by age group (Adolescents, Adults, All ages), sex (Male only, Female only, Both), and client characteristic (AIDS, Criminal, Homeless, Mentally ill, Pregnant, Spanish speaking). All dots appear in the "Both" sex columns; the "Male only" and "Female only" columns contain no entries.

Program	Adolescents — Both						Adults — Both						All ages — Both[1]					
	AIDS	Criminal	Homeless	Mentally ill	Pregnant	Spanish speaking	AIDS	Criminal	Homeless	Mentally ill	Pregnant	Spanish speaking	AIDS	Criminal	Homeless	Mentally ill	Pregnant	Spanish speaking
06-2 Essex Substance Abuse Treatment Center, Inc., Newark[4]													●	●	●	●	●	●
08-4 Integrity House, Inc., Newark							●	●	●		●							
08-5 Integrity House, Inc., Newark[5]		●																
08-6 Integrity House, Inc., Newark[5]																		
09-1 La Casa Don Pedro, Newark													●	●				●
09-3 La Casa Don Pedro, Newark					●													●
09-2 La Casa Don Pedro, Newark[5]													●	●				
13-3 Newark Renaissance House, Newark							●	●	●	●	●							
19-2 Turning Point, Inc., Newark							●	●	●	●	●	●						
20-1 United Community Corp., Newark							●	●	●		●	●						
20-2 United Community Corp., Newark							●	●	●		●	●						
22-1 UMDNJ Alcohol Treatment Center, Newark							●	●	●		●	●						

[1] Some programs restrict minimum age to mid-adolescent or older
[2] Ages 17 and over
[3] Juveniles under special circumstances
[4] Substance abuser and family members (including children)
[5] Alcohol only

RAND#6623-4.1c-0993

Legend for category columns within each age/sex block:
AIDS, Crim = Criminal, Home = Homeless, MI = Mentally ill, Preg = Pregnant, Span = Spanish speaking. (Male-only blocks have no "Pregnant" column.)

Program	Adolescents — Male only					Adolescents — Female only						Adolescents — Both						Adults — Male only					Adults — Female only						Adults — Both						All ages — Male only					All ages — Female only						All ages — Both					
	AIDS	Crim	Home	MI	Span	AIDS	Crim	Home	MI	Preg	Span	AIDS	Crim	Home	MI	Preg	Span	AIDS	Crim	Home	MI	Span	AIDS	Crim	Home	MI	Preg	Span	AIDS	Crim	Home	MI	Preg	Span	AIDS	Crim	Home	MI	Span	AIDS	Crim	Home	MI	Preg	Span	AIDS	Crim	Home	MI	Preg	Span
Rehab—day program																																																			
02-4 Catholic Community Services, Newark																													●	●	●	●	●	●																	
08-2 Integrity Inc., Newark												●	●	●																																					
13-2 Newark Renaissance House, Newark												●	●	●																																					
27-2 East Orange General Hospital, East Orange																													●					●																	
Rehab—inpatient/residential																																																			
04-1 CURA, Inc., Newark[5]																													●	●	●	●	●																	
04-3 CURA, Inc., Newark		●																																																	
04-4 CURA, Inc., Newark				●																									●	●				●																	
08-1 Integrity Inc., Newark		●	●																										●					●																	
08-3 Integrity Inc., Newark																													●	●	●																				
13-1 Newark Renaissance House, Newark	●	●	●																										●	●	●	●																			
19-1 Turning Point, Inc., Verona																													●		●																				
23-1 VA Medical Center, East Orange																													●		●																				
23-2 VA Medical Center, East Orange																													●		●																				

[1] Some programs restrict minimum age to mid-adolescent or older
[2] Ages 17 and over
[3] Juveniles under special circumstances
[4] Substance abuser and family members (including children)
[5] Alcohol only

Figure 4.1—continued

RAND#623-4.1d-0993

Adolescents

Program	Male only: AIDS	Male only: Criminal	Male only: Homeless	Male only: Mentally ill	Male only: Spanish speaking	Female only: AIDS	Female only: Criminal	Female only: Homeless	Female only: Mentally ill	Female only: Pregnant	Female only: Spanish speaking	Both: AIDS	Both: Criminal	Both: Homeless	Both: Mentally ill	Both: Pregnant	Both: Spanish speaking
Rehab—inpatient/residential																	
26-1 Straight & Narrow, Inc., Paterson						●	●	●	●								
26-2 Straight & Narrow, Inc., Paterson	●	●	●	●													
26-3 Straight & Narrow, Inc., Paterson																	
26-4 Straight & Narrow, Inc., Paterson																	
Aftercare/reentry																	
02-3 Catholic Community Services, Newark																	
03-1 Choices, Inc., Newark[4]																	
08-7 Integrity Inc., Newark																	
09-4 La Casa De Don Pedro, Newark																	●
25-1 Volunteers of America, Newark																	
27-3 East Orange General Hospital, East Orange																	

Adults

Program	Male only: AIDS	Male only: Criminal	Male only: Homeless	Male only: Mentally ill	Male only: Spanish speaking	Female only: AIDS	Female only: Criminal	Female only: Homeless	Female only: Mentally ill	Female only: Pregnant	Female only: Spanish speaking	Both: AIDS	Both: Criminal	Both: Homeless	Both: Mentally ill	Both: Pregnant	Both: Spanish speaking
Rehab—inpatient/residential																	
26-1 Straight & Narrow, Inc., Paterson																	
26-2 Straight & Narrow, Inc., Paterson																	
26-3 Straight & Narrow, Inc., Paterson	●	●	●	●													
26-4 Straight & Narrow, Inc., Paterson						●	●	●	●	●							
Aftercare/reentry																	
02-3 Catholic Community Services, Newark	●	●	●	●	●												
03-1 Choices, Inc., Newark[4]						●	●	●		●							
08-7 Integrity Inc., Newark		●			●												
09-4 La Casa De Don Pedro, Newark																	
25-1 Volunteers of America, Newark		●															
27-3 East Orange General Hospital, East Orange												●	●	●		●	

All ages

Program	Male only: AIDS	Male only: Criminal	Male only: Homeless	Male only: Mentally ill	Male only: Spanish speaking	Female only: AIDS	Female only: Criminal	Female only: Homeless	Female only: Mentally ill	Female only: Pregnant	Female only: Spanish speaking	Both: AIDS	Both: Criminal	Both: Homeless	Both: Mentally ill	Both: Pregnant	Both: Spanish speaking
Rehab—inpatient/residential																	
26-1 Straight & Narrow, Inc., Paterson																	
26-2 Straight & Narrow, Inc., Paterson																	
26-3 Straight & Narrow, Inc., Paterson																	
26-4 Straight & Narrow, Inc., Paterson																	
Aftercare/reentry																	
02-3 Catholic Community Services, Newark																	
03-1 Choices, Inc., Newark[4]																	
08-7 Integrity Inc., Newark																	
09-4 La Casa De Don Pedro, Newark																	
25-1 Volunteers of America, Newark																	
27-3 East Orange General Hospital, East Orange																	

[1]Some programs restrict minimum age to mid-adolescent or older
[2]Ages 17 and over
[3]Juveniles under special circumstances
[4]Substance abuser and family members (including children)
[5]Alcohol only

Figure 4.1—continued

RAND#623-4.2-0993

Type of program	Adolescent only	Adolescent males only	Adolescent females only	Adults only	Adult males only	Adult females only	Criminal justice referrals	Department of Corrections	Veterans	Spanish speakers	Mentally ill
Methadone maintenance									23-3		
Total capacity									*230*		
Inpatient detox				15-1 02-1 27-1					23-4		
Total capacity				*58*							
Outpatient detox									*15*		
Rehab—outpatient	09-3			20-1, 2 19-2, 22-1 13-3, 02-2 08-4, 09-1, 2			08-5 08-6			04-2	
Total capacity	*10*			*2,356*			*85*			*124*	
Rehab—day programs	13-2 08-2			27-2							
Total capacity	*60*			*55*							
Rehab—inpatient/ residential		26-2 13-1 08-1	26-1	19-1 08-3	26-3	26-4			23-2 23-1	04-4 04-3 04-1	02-4
Total capacity		*80*	*10*	*250*	*35*	*155*			*47*	*112*	*50*
Aftercare re-entry	09-4			27-3	02-3	03-1		25-1 08-7			
Total capacity	*30*			*130*	*36*	*36*		*166*			

SOURCE: RAND inventory, 1991.

NOTE: Numbers on chart refer to the provider and program name shown in Figure 4.1.

Figure 4.2—Programs Restricted to Specific Populations

The other bad news is that the overall treatment capacity is less than it seems, when restrictions are considered. For example, four of 47 programs were limited to veterans only. The methadone maintenance program for veterans reported a capacity of 230, and a current caseload of 99, leaving its excess capacity unavailable to other demand populations.

Another way to identify resources for specific groups is to look within programs and determine whether they specialize in treatment for specific groups while offering treatment to a broader group. Figure 4.3 shows the population groups for which programs offered special services. In this figure, we see that several programs specialized in treatment for pregnant women, AIDS patients, the mentally ill, the homeless, criminal justice system referrals, and Spanish speakers. For example, there were detoxification, outpatient, day-care, and residential rehabilitation and reentry programs that specialize in treatment for pregnant women. Seventeen programs specialized in substance abuse treatment for people with AIDS, and seven offered special treatment for the dually diagnosed mentally ill. However, in all of these programs, these special needs groups competed for treatment slots with larger populations also served by the program.

Utilization

As shown in Table 4.2, programs differed in the extent to which they operated at, above, or below their capacity. This is true within all of the modality and environment combinations except reentry, where all six programs for which we have information reported operating at capacity. All of the reentry providers reported waiting lists for their programs, suggesting a large unmet demand for this type of program.

Programs in other modalities also sometimes reported waiting lists as of January 1, 1991. For example, one methadone maintenance program serving about 700 clients had a waiting list of 50. Among outpatient programs, most that could give us information over the phone said they had no waiting lists, but these programs sometimes expand capacity to meet demand. The residential rehabilitation programs that reported on waiting lists told us that the waiting list was at least equal to their total capacity.

Interpreting waiting list information is difficult, because we are not sure what it says about demand for treatment and because list-keeping is different for every program. It would help to know something about the characteristics of people on waiting lists and what happens to them after they get on a list. For example, they may be on multiple lists, they may be on one list and in treatment

RAND#623-4.3-0993

Type of program	Pregnant women	AIDS patients	Mentally ill	Homeless	Criminal justice referrals	Veterans	Spanish speakers
Methadone maintenance		23-3	18-1	23-3	18-1, 23-3	23-3	
Inpatient detox		15-1		23-4 15-1		23-4	15-1
Outpatient detox	6-1	6-1	18-2		18-2		6-1
Rehab—outpatient	13-3, 20-1 3-2, 6-2	13-3, 20-2 3-2, 4-2, 6-2 9-1		20-1 20-2 8-4, 22-1	20-1 20-2 8-4, 6-2 8-5 8-6 9-2		4-2 9-1, 3
Rehab—day program	19-2	19-2 2-4	19-2 2-4	19-2			2-4
Rehab—inpatient/residential	19-1 26-4 (and neonates)	4-1, 4, 19-1 23-1, 2	19-1 23-1, 2	19-1 23-1, 2		23-1, 2	4-3, 4
Aftercare re-entry	3-1	3-1			25-1 8-7		9-4

SOURCE: RAND inventory, 1991.

NOTE: Numbers on chart refer to the provider and program name shown in Figure 4.1.

Figure 4.3—Programs Specializing in the Treatment of Particular Groups

Table 4.2

Utilization of Inventoried Providers

	Total Inventoried	Programs at Capacity	Programs Above Capacity	Programs Below Capacity	N/A
Methadone maintenance	2	1		1	0
Inpatient detox	5	1		4	0
Outpatient detox	2	2			0
Rehab—outpatient	15	3	2	8	2
Rehab—day programs	4		2	1	1
Rehab—inpatient/ residential	13	9	1	3	0
Aftercare/reentry	6	6			0

SOURCE: RAND Inventory, 1991.

somewhere else, or they may have changed their minds entirely about seeking treatment.

Part of the reason some programs operate under maximum capacity is that they are restricted to certain groups. Others may be at less than capacity because of the higher costs of treatment (e.g., inpatient detoxification programs) or their location. A more detailed analysis of capacity and utilization would be necessary to identify the areas of greatest unmet demand.

Not surprisingly, when asked about the need for additional treatment capacity, providers agreed that much additional capacity was needed. But they also disagreed about where the greatest unmet need existed. However, inpatient detoxification, long-term residential rehabilitation, and intensive day programs were noted most frequently as the treatment environments and modalities that should be increased in capacity, and most agreed that there was not a lot of unmet need for additional methadone maintenance capacity.

Substances Treated

Most program directors we interviewed pointed out the need to be able to treat both alcohol and drug problems, due to the high prevalence of both problems among the treatment population. Even programs set up to treat only alcoholism were providing other substance abuse treatment to meet the needs of those who were using alcohol and drugs in combination. As a consequence, we found very few programs that were only treating alcohol or drug abuse. While the methadone programs, by definition, are limited to heroin treatment, most other programs did not specialize in substances, again probably because of the high prevalence of polydrug use among their clientele. For example, we found no cocaine-only program.

Program Features

The program duration varies both within and across program types. Inpatient detoxification programs require only several days to complete treatment, while many outpatient programs are designed to provide care indefinitely. In Newark, about half the residential rehabilitation programs are short term, and about half require stays from six to twelve months. Table 4.3 shows the range of program durations for each type of program and the average length of stay in a program, as reported by providers. The latter information is often not available from providers, because discharge or termination records are difficult to keep, especially for clients who drop out of programs or, in the case of outpatient programs, attend very intermittently.

Table 4.4 shows how many programs offered collateral services, such as medical care, AIDS counseling, transportation, education assistance, employment assistance, child care, and counseling for children of substance abusers. It shows quite a bit of variation among programs in the services they offered. Some features are more relevant to certain programs than to others, and the absence of a certain feature may have more to do with the population served than anything else. For example, programs for adolescent boys are much less likely to need to provide child care than are programs for adults.

Most providers agreed that the need for these services in addition to substance abuse treatment was great. Medical care, AIDS counseling, and child care were named most frequently as the most important targets for increased collateral services for the treatment population.

Table 4.3
Program Duration and Length of Stay

	Program Duration	Average Length of Stay
Inpatient detox	2–14 days	5–15 days
Outpatient detox	21–180 days	90 days
Rehab—outpatient	Most have no fixed length	6 @ 3–6 months 5 @ 9–12 months
Rehab—inpatient/ residential	7 @ 90 days or less 6 @ 6–12 months	n.a.
Aftercare/reentry	3–12 months	2.5 –12 months

SOURCE: RAND Inventory, 1991.

Table 4.4

Collateral Services Offered by Treatment Providers

	Methadone Maintenance	Inpatient Detox	Outpatient Detox	Outpatient	Day	Residential	Reentry
Total programs included in count	2	5	2	15	4	13	6
AIDS counseling	2	3	2	10	4	12	2
Child care	1	3	1	1			
Counseling for children of substance abusers	6	2	1				
Education assistance	1	2	9	1			
Employment assistance	7	2	9	5			
Leave policy	1	10	3				
Meals	1	3					
Medical care	1	5	1	3	2	13	
Psychiatric care	2	1	1	3			
Assistance for Spanish speakers	2	2	2	7	2	2	
Transportation	1	1	1				
Other services volunteered							
Methadone maintenance	1	1					
Rehab component	1						
Aftercare	7	1					
Recreation	1						
Housing	4						

SOURCE: RAND inventory, 1991.

If information could be gathered about the populations served by independent providers of collateral services, such as the Work Oriented Rehabilitation Institute (WORI) and the Boarder and Abandoned Babies Intervention, Education and Supplemental Services (BABIES) program, it could be used to facilitate referral from treatment providers to the organizations that provide services such as those listed in Table 4.4.[4] As discussed below, the absence of some of these services, such as child care (offered by few programs), is sometimes a serious barrier to entering treatment.

Unmet Demand and Barriers to Treatment

As noted above, it is difficult to determine unmet need from the limited capacity utilization and waiting list information currently available. What is needed is a far better estimate of the population in need of treatment based on information about the extent of substance abuse and dependence in different populations. Newark does not have some of the basic tools that are used elsewhere in the country to estimate this population. It has no survey of substance use to capture the prevalence of high-rate users and the problems they have as a result of substance use. It also lacks a broad-based survey of use among youth, including school dropouts. Finally, the Drug Use Forecasting (DUF) system, which is used to estimate rates of drug use among arrestees, does not collect data in Newark. However, estimates of the number of heavy drug users alone are insufficient to calculate the demand for treatment in a community. Rate of demand is, almost certainly, also a function of the level of outreach, ability to pay, and incentives and obstacles to entering a program.

The information we gathered from the providers we surveyed sheds some light on where additional treatment resources could be used in Newark. For example, there are few programs for females; our respondents noted the need for more, including services for women with special conditions or problems (e.g., pregnant women, battered women, sexually abused women, and women who have turned to prostitution to support their drug habits).

Also, few programs are able to arrange for child care. Some of the providers we surveyed noted how difficult a barrier this can be for a mother entering treatment, especially long-term residential treatment. Some mothers, for example, bring their young children with them to the methadone clinics because they have no place to leave them. One provider, which offers meals as part of its

---

[4]See Appendix A for a partial list of these organizations.

program, noted that some mothers are accompanied by children who should be in school; since the mothers cannot afford to pay for a school lunch, they bring the children with them because they can get a meal for them at the clinic. Although the new BABIES program in Newark is designed to provide housing for "boarder babies" and babies whose mothers are in substance abuse treatment, outreach to women considering treatment could be improved if child-care facilities were more available.

One population group for which there were few special treatment services at the time of our inventory is the elderly. A number of our respondents mentioned the problems of overmedication in this population and of alcohol problems that result from being homebound. Only one program in Newark provided services for substance abuse problems among older people.

Other barriers to entering long-term residential rehabilitation programs often cannot be overcome. For example, some people would lose their homes while participating in a residential rehabilitation treatment program. Public housing regulations require that units be occupied, making it impossible for many in public housing, who have waited for years to get an apartment and who cannot afford alternative housing, to consider long-term residential treatment, even if they could get in. If more such programs had leave policies or home visit provisions, greater numbers of public housing tenants might be able to participate without losing their apartments. This problem might also be overcome if capacity in intensive day programs were expanded.

Another logistical barrier is posed to those who are employed, even if only on a part-time basis. When entering residential programs, people who work often face the loss of their jobs. Some providers told us that outpatient programs need to have more flexible hours to accommodate clients who have jobs.

While providers had many perspectives on the barriers to treatment, the majority believed that the most important barrier was the lack of adequate funding for indigent care. Many respondents noted the lack of aftercare services for their clients. They say that after their detoxification or rehabilitation program, they have no choice but to turn the patients back out into the same environment where they developed their drug problem. There is also a need for more programs like the WORI.

In addition to aftercare, several people pointed out the need for more effective outreach that facilitates getting people who are seeking help into a program. Some lose interest because they must wait for access. Others cannot get through the bureaucracy of applications and screening processes on their own. For example, some programs require that clients obtain medical and/or psychological exams or clearances before they can be accepted, but the treatment program does not provide this service. Fulfilling numerous requirements before entering treatment can be difficult and defeating. This is another area where a clearinghouse could be helpful, identifying what is needed to be accepted by a program and facilitating completion of the screening requirements.

Substance Abuse Prevention

Interventions developed to reduce or prevent substance abuse have taken many forms, including school-based prevention/education programs, mass media campaigns, youth clubs and activities designed as alternatives to substance use, and community-based programs. Evaluations of these efforts indicate that these interventions have (1) frequently increased knowledge and awareness about substance abuse problems, and (2) occasionally had an impact on attitudes toward substance abuse and related issues. However, rarely have any of these interventions been shown to have had an impact on actual substance use behavior (Botvin, 1990).

A major exception is a class of school-based primary prevention approaches that focus on the key psychosocial factors that appear to promote substance use among adolescents. These approaches include either resistance-skills training alone or in combination with life-skills training. One such model, developed and tested by RAND, was shown to have reduced initiation of marijuana use among students in middle schools where the program was tested by one-third, compared to students who did not receive the training (Ellickson and Bell, 1990). One of the principal conclusions of the experiment was that periodic booster sessions are needed to maintain the effects of the intervention.

Many diverse organizations in Newark are involved in a great variety of education, prevention training, counseling, intervention, and referral programs. Public agencies, such as the Newark Board of Education and the Essex County Prosecutor, play a role, as well as many private organizations, churches, and community groups. We quickly determined that our needs assessment could not possibly identify all such programs in Newark without a great deal more resources than we had. We also learned of another needs assessment focused specifically on substance abuse prevention, being undertaken by the Newark Department of Health. Therefore, our discussion of prevention programs is limited to an overview, and because of NFB's special interest in youth, we focus primarily on the range of activities concerned with substance abuse in the Newark schools.

School-Based Prevention Programs

All grades, kindergarten through twelve, receive some drug education instruction in the Newark public schools. New Jersey law specifies that "the nature of alcoholic drinks and narcotics and their effects upon the human system shall be taught in all schools . . . in such manner as may be adapted to the age and understanding of the pupils and shall be emphasized in appropriate places of the curriculum sufficiently for a full and adequate treatment of the subject."[5] State regulation requires 10 hours of classroom training based on curriculum guidelines contained in the grade-specific Drug Education Curriculum Guide. The Dave Winfield Foundation "Turning Around" curriculum is also used in some schools. However, according to the Newark School Board's Drug Education Supervisor, these tools serve only as guidelines for the classroom teachers, who tone the message to the level of their classes. No empirical evaluation of Newark's classroom-based prevention education has been conducted.

Drug education in Newark is coordinated by the School Board's Drug Education Supervisor. The School Board requires each school principal to form a Drug Review Committee at the beginning of each year. The committee reviews the curriculum guide and evaluates each student involved in drug and alcohol abuse incidents. The committee is composed of the principal or his designee, the school social worker or psychologist, a staff member of a drug treatment agency approved by the School Board, the school nurse, a concerned parent, and, if necessary, a law enforcement representative. Each school-level committee is convened by the school's Substance Awareness Coordinator (SAC). There are 18 SACs assigned to cover Newark's 80 public schools.

The SACs are 10-month employees of the District, recruited from the teaching staff. They are based in the highest-risk schools and assigned an additional four schools each. There is a SAC present in each middle school and most senior high schools. According to the Drug Education Supervisor, there is increasing need to base SACs in some elementary schools, but not enough positions exist. The SACs are responsible for classroom substance awareness teaching (spending 7 hours per week in classroom sessions, as assigned by school principals), intervention with individual schools, and referral of pupils to treatment resources.

In January 1991, the Board of Education began using Drug Free Schools funds to offer training to school teams dealing with substance awareness. This training

---

[5]New Jersey Statutes, 18A:35-4.

brings together the school's SAC, psychologist or social worker, nurse, physical education teacher, and principal (or designee) for three-day training sessions on working as a team to handle substance awareness education and individual pupil problems at each school.

In October 1990, the Board began to recruit Positive Alternatives Counselors (PACs), usually school guidance counselors, to organize clubs at elementary schools for students in grades 4–8. The purpose of the clubs is to offer pupils interesting activities that serve as positive alternatives to substance abuse. An example of PAC activities was a half-day youth conference held at the University of Medicine and Dentistry of New Jersey, which featured various entertainment acts, celebrities, and experts who provided information about drugs and substance abuse to 300 students from Newark elementary schools. By early 1991, there were PACs in 35 of 80 schools. However, funding for this program, like the SACs, is limited to the months of the school year. The Newark schools have no summer programs in substance abuse education for their students.

Community-Based Programs

Many organizations sponsor substance abuse education, intervention, and referral. In Newark, several churches have taken a lead in this area, coordinated by The Black Churchmen's United Drug Task Force. The National Black Alcoholism Council is an example of a private organization that provides professionally trained speakers and counselors to community audiences and groups. The International Youth Organization in Newark offers educational programs aimed at youth. Many other private organizations, some of which are listed in Appendix E, are involved in prevention education. However, this effort is not well coordinated citywide.

School- and Community-Based Programs

The new Newark Cluster Schools program offers an opportunity to combine school and community messages about substance awareness and substance abuse education. In early 1991, the Cluster Schools program was planning a Parents Academy, designed to provide parenting training and other education for parents of its school youth. This is the kind of vehicle that could be used to extend the prevention messages taught in school into the pupils' homes and communities.

5. Drug Markets and Drug Law Enforcement in Newark

In January of 1990, the Director of the Office of National Drug Control Policy designated five areas nationwide as "high intensity drug trafficking areas."[1] The metropolitan area of New York was one of them, and Essex County was specifically included as part of the New York high-intensity area.

Most of the local law enforcement efforts devoted to reducing the use of drugs in Newark are targeted at disrupting "street markets" (locations where dealers congregate to sell drugs) and on arresting individual street-level dealers.[2] The eventual success of law enforcement in reducing the flow of drugs into Newark, or at least in making it more difficult for inexperienced buyers to obtain drugs on the streets, will require improved information on the characteristics of drug dealers and the methods they use to operate.

In this section, we first summarize the findings from exploratory research on drug dealers and their marketing methods derived from personal interviews with 16 young men and women recently involved in selling drugs in Newark.[3] We then examine the arrest and disposition data for a sample of drug sellers arrested by the NPD.

How Young Sellers Characterize Local Drug Markets

According to the young men and one of the two women we interviewed, it would be simplistic and misleading to characterize drug distribution in Newark as one market: There appear to be a number of markets, highly decentralized and operating very much as entrepreneurial street-level retail scenes. Each neighborhood appears to have its own market that functions independently from

---

[1]National Drug Control Strategy (White House, 1991).

[2]Efforts by DEA and the Sheriff's Narcotics Unit are directed more toward identifying and gathering evidence on mid- and higher-level dealers. In 1990, the U.S. Drug Enforcement Agency (DEA) had more than 300 Class 1 cases (criminal organizations with five or more people involved) active in Newark.

[3]The interviews were conducted by graduate students from the School of Criminal Justice at Rutgers University in April and May of 1991. The respondents were adolescent males from Ogden House, a juvenile correction facility in Newark, and male and female probationers referred by the Essex County Probation Department. The respondents were between 16 and 25 years of age. Most had been selling drugs for a few years before the interview. All but one respondent were African American; the other was Puerto Rican. The interviews lasted about two hours each.

others. Moreover, "neighborhoods" are defined in very small units—usually block faces or corners.

Street-level drug sellers we had the opportunity to interview were young, and, although they reported a wide age range among sellers they knew, most, not surprisingly, said there were few people older than 30 who were selling drugs.

Cocaine, either in rock or powder form, is the most widely sold drug. It is sold in units that cost $10 or $20 (equivalent to about $100 per gram of cocaine). There appears to be little demand for crack, the smokable form of cocaine. Among the sellers we interviewed, there was little wholesale selling; most buyers bought three or four "dimes" ($10 units packaged in small glass bottles) at a time. The pattern of selling and using, in fact, closely resembles the vast street-level market that operated in the Lower East Side of New York City in the years preceding crack (the early 1980s). And, as we see below, the distribution chain itself leaves little opportunity for selling in higher quantities.

Supply and Distribution

New York City is a major entry point for cocaine in the United States, and it is clear that the Newark cocaine market is a subsidiary market for the New York distribution networks. However, there appears to be little wholesale or "upper-level" cocaine distribution in Newark or Essex County, as evidenced by the absence of large seizures of drugs in Newark arrests. There has been much speculation by regional DEA officials that cocaine entering through the Port of Newark bypasses local distributors and goes directly to importers in New York or other major cities.[4]

The few Newark cocaine sellers we interviewed seemed to be wholly dependent on New York suppliers for their product; all of the cocaine sellers we interviewed obtained their product from New York City. They went to the city once a week or more, typically spending $1,000 to $1,500 per trip, buying about a half ounce of cocaine. Most reported that they doubled their money: $1,500 of cocaine purchased in New York would yield a retail gross of $3,000 to $4,000 on Newark's streets.

One respondent described his first trip to New York to buy drugs. He had heard that the corner of 145th Street between Lenox and Amsterdam avenues was a good place to buy something. With $1,500 in his pocket, and knowing no one, he traveled by PATH and the subway to that location. Amid the busy street traffic

---

[4]Interview with Robert Stutman, former director of the New York Regional DEA office, 1989.

in drugs, he heard someone hawking a brand name he knew; he simply approached the person and made a buy.

We also interviewed a female heroin seller and a woman who sold a wide range of drugs: marijuana and prescription drugs (codeine, various tranquilizers such as Valium, etc.) stolen from a pharmaceutical company. Most cocaine sellers also sold marijuana. In fact, selling marijuana was the one constant that was common to the drug markets in Newark. Some reported that selling marijuana was their entry into drug selling; others specialized in marijuana.

In contrast to the street markets in New York City neighborhoods, drug selling in Newark lacks formal organization. It appears for the most part to be an individual entrepreneurial system. Few of the dealers reported working in gangs, organizations, or crews. Their evolution into entrepreneurs was not unlike that of other businessmen or businesswomen. Most started out working for someone else before going out on their own. Most bought their product and distributed it themselves; only one worked on consignment.

If there were groups, they were generally loose business affiliations where friends might pool their money to buy larger quantities at a discount and perhaps serve as lookouts for each other to guard against robberies or trouble from the police. One of the dealers worked in a group of nine—three minicrews of three sellers each. Only one of those we interviewed worked in what might be characterized as a true organization—an elaborate network of 40 people selling heroin.

The Customers

Most sellers recognized customers from their neighborhoods, and each presented a distinct profile of his or her customers. However, these profiles were quite varied. Buyers were mostly African Americans, but there were also some whites. Buyers included males and females from all social classes. Some reported that working people in readily identifiable trucks or vans would pull up to a curbside location and buy during work hours. The buyers seemed to represent a wide cross section of working people in Newark.

The bulk of the dealers' income came from regular customers who would buy 3 to 4 dimes each day; occasional buyers were not a large share of the market. The sellers tried to know their customers to minimize risk. They were leery of strangers, and some said they would test a new customer by pulling a gun on him or her and looking for a reaction of fear. Although each respondent denied selling to adolescents or children, they all claimed to know a dealer who did.

Times and Locations

Much of the drug selling activity undertaken by those we interviewed occurs in public: Street-level drug selling is commonplace in several Newark neighborhoods, generally outdoors at curbside or pedestrian markets, or indoors at informal social gatherings. Both of the females interviewed sold in front of their houses. Some of the males sold in alleyways, others sold while walking streets busy with pedestrian traffic. Some sold on street corners, and still others sold from houses.

Although the dealers said some times were better (more active) than others, there was little agreement on which times of day produced the most buyers. This is not surprising, since those we talked with sold at different times of day. But there were peak selling days that most dealers recognized: generally paydays and days when welfare checks were issued.

Violence and Drug Selling

Drug markets have been typified as ruthless milieus where disputes are settled with violence and where both buyers and sellers are targets for robbery. Some studies have shown that violent people dominate these markets and that only those with violent skills can function effectively. Newark sellers did report that the risk of violence was considerable. Most had been robbed of their money or drugs at one time or another. Two were beaten up, and one had been shot at by the police on more than one occasion.

The active and entrepreneurial drug market also seems to have spawned new careers in robbery: Several sellers reported that they had been robbed by "stickup boys," small crews of young men who specialize in robbing drug dealers. The stickup boys appear to be a more violent group than the sellers, although the sellers may have understated their own violence.

We interviewed two young men who described themselves as stickup boys. They told similar stories, despite being from different neighborhoods and unknown to each other. Both had been former street sellers of cocaine who grew weary of the "long grind" of cold nights on street corners, dealing with the public. They thought that street-level sellers were "chumps" for standing outside in the cold and rain, taking all night to make a few hundred dollars. They saw robbery as a faster way to make the same money, with little perceived risk.

They and their crews operated in cars, singling out lone sellers as robbery targets. They would stop the car next to the seller, jump out and surround him, show their weapons (usually handguns or sawed-off rifles), take his money and drugs, and quickly escape. They claimed to make about $1,000 per active night for each of them (a crew of three). They did not fear a struggle from their victims: They said that sellers were reluctant to carry weapons for fear of the additional burden in court of a gun charge under the Graves Act. They also did not fear reprisal, since they rarely operated in the same neighborhood in which they lived and were strangers to their victims.

The stickup boys, too, described the drug selling system as a freelance market with little organization or discipline. Accordingly, they had no fear of reprisals from others within an "organization." When asked whether the robbed victims were at some risk of reprisal from suppliers, they said that sellers usually had to pay for their "stash" up front.

Thus Newark's active but disorganized cocaine market has generated an additional criminal industry for those willing to ply violence and undertake the limited risk of either reprisal or the added criminal liability of a weapons charge.

Characteristics of Drug Sellers

Family Backgrounds

Most of those interviewed were raised by their mothers and siblings, and two had children of their own. Their family economic and educational backgrounds portray blue-collar families that range from "working poor" to "comfortable though modest economic means." These young dealers did not come from severely distressed families living in poverty. Their parents generally were high school graduates, and the parents of two of the respondents had college degrees. One father was a manager in a company, another worked for the city of Newark. Mothers' work ranged from fast-food service for the Board of Education to restaurant work.

The respondents were somewhat defensive or embarrassed to talk about the experience of their family members with the law enforcement community. Most who had siblings indicated that at least one of their siblings had been in trouble with the law or had been incarcerated at some time. In some cases, a sibling had been instrumental in bringing the respondent into the drug trade.

Participation in Legitimate Work

Recent research on drug sellers in New York, Boston, and Washington, D.C., has suggested that about half of those who sell drugs are working legitimate jobs at the same time (Reuter, MacCoun, and Murphy, 1990). This has important policy implications, since redirecting these young people to licit jobs may not be sufficient to dissuade them from selling drugs. About half of the Newark sellers were working or had worked recently, although their attachments to the labor force were weak at best. Part-time work was more common than full-time employment—one man took home about $50 per week working at odd jobs. The two women worked full time as clerks at a local retail store; two of the men worked at a sandwich shop. The women took home between $150 and $180 per week, a fraction of their drug incomes. Others reported income from unemployment insurance, support from family (about $100 to $200 per month), or friends, and one reported "hustling" for about $25 per month (panhandling, returning bottles).

Education

Most had little education other than high school and were unlikely to obtain well-paying jobs. Only one of the young men at Ogden House had completed high school, although many said they planned to get GEDs. Although the probationers had graduated from high school, most had been suspended at least once. One probationer had two years of college, but he clearly was the exception.

Criminal Records

The females had only one or two arrests, far fewer than the males. Most of the males had prior drug arrests; a few had burglary, stolen property, and fraud (bad checks, forgery) charges. Only one person reported a prior robbery arrest. In general, violence was rare among this group, but it may have been a reflection of the sample. One interviewer observed that the more intelligent young men were better businessmen and better able to avoid arrest.

Getting Started

Money was the motivation for getting into drug selling. The respondents started selling in mid- to late adolescence and had been selling for several years. They all were envious of the money and displays of wealth they saw among other dealers, including in some cases family members. One person said he saw how other drug dealers lived, especially their "materialism." One young man said he started selling because he had spent money designated for sneakers in a video arcade. He borrowed drugs from a friend to recoup the sneaker money, made $1,000 his first day, and never stopped selling until he was arrested.

Most were introduced casually into drug selling by family or friends, but "easy money" was the motive for getting more deeply involved. The respondents said that they became accustomed to the money and wanted to maintain their income. They generally started selling for a friend for a few months before going out on their own. The two females both got started through a male friend who was their first connection. One continued to sell for that man, while the other went out on her own.

There was little that was mysterious about getting started. Unlike sellers in other recent studies, the Newark sellers we interviewed did not "drift" into selling. It happened rather purposefully and within a somewhat short time span. None expressed any ambivalence (other than risk) about having gotten involved.

Locations

Most sellers claimed to avoid selling in their own neighborhoods. None said that they sold while working at legal jobs. They disliked the neighborhoods where they lived and were highly critical (perhaps disingenuously so) of the drug traffic and violence in their neighborhoods. Many mentioned that Stratford Place was the roughest neighborhood in Newark, with an active and violent drug market.

The sellers tended to seek out fairly pleasant places to sell, avoiding areas with abandoned buildings or hulks of stolen cars. One said he liked to sell in a "nice area, like a suburb." Whether this was a business or an aesthetic decision was unclear. However, since many admitted knowing or recognizing their customers from their neighborhoods, it is likely that they sometimes sold drugs near home or only a short distance away.

Income

Since they were only occasional participants in licit work, most of the respondents reported that drug selling was their primary source of income. A few also engaged in other crimes for income (e.g., car theft, burglary), and one gambled. Only the stickup boys made their money from violence.

There has been much speculation about how much money drug dealers make. Depending on whether one asks about the net or gross income, estimates from drug sellers vary widely. Several studies suggest that street-level sellers net an hourly wage of about $30 for each active hour worked (Reuter et al., 1990; Viscusi, 1986). Selling does not occur on a regular 8-hour, 5-day-per-week schedule. It is really an occasional type of work. Some of the dealers sold in 8- to 12-hour shifts, others sold for much shorter periods. Some sold daily, others sold less frequently. One female and one male said they sold seven days a week. One male cocaine seller said he was on call 24 hours a day, 7 days a week, and sold whenever there was any demand. When asked about the frequencies and amounts of selling, we heard these various responses:

- The female heroin seller sold 40 $15 bags a day, four days per week, and 15 $10 bags of marijuana per day.

- The female marijuana seller sold one-half pound per day. Marijuana retails at over $2,500 per pound when broken down into smaller units (dimes, ounces, and half ounces).

- One cocaine seller claimed to have sold 90 $10 "caps" (bottles) per day every day, as well as 1/4 pound of marijuana.

- A marijuana seller sold loose joints, in various numbers, for about three days each week, depending on how much he could afford to buy at one time.

Estimates of typical daily gross incomes ranged from $300 to $1,200 per day, with a median of about $800. The problem in estimating weekly or monthly incomes is in figuring out how many days a week the typical sellers worked. Each of them reported making one or two trips a week into New York to acquire drugs, typically in $1,000 bulk quantities that they then repackaged and sold for twice as much. Regular weekly trips of this nature would earn them gross monthly incomes on the order of $8,000 to $16,000 per month. The problem lies in estimating the regularity of these trips, and how long they were kept up. None of the dealers we talked with had been in business for more than a year. Many had only been selling for just a few months. It may be that their high rates of activity are what led them to be incarcerated as juveniles and that many other dealers operate at considerably less volume. None of them could account for spending anything like $8,000 to 10,000 per month.

The sellers' incomes were sufficient to support what was for them an opulent lifestyle: Most spent their money on jewelry, clothes, entertainment, cars (one male said he bought three cars in one year), and gifts for girlfriends. They also gave money and gifts to their families and expressed much pride in this. None of them considered saving any of their earnings.

Drug Use

Most of the dealers said they were careful to avoid excessive drug use. None were selling to support their own habits, and their use did not increase after their income and access to drugs increased. Most smoked marijuana, some occasionally, two very often. Cocaine use was rare, as was the use of pills (one reported occasional Seconal use) or hallucinogens (one female used mescaline occasionally). Both females said they had been addicted to heroin, and one went to treatment while the other stopped without treatment. They also said their friends used heroin. Their involvement in a heroin network where cocaine use is infrequent resembles patterns observed in New York where cocaine and crack networks are quite separate from heroin networks. Alcohol use was common to all sellers but at low frequencies.

The males looked down on their customers; the females did not. Given the womens' patterns of heroin use and selling, this is not surprising, since selling and using apparently were comingled socially and economically. However, the male cocaine sellers described their customers as "fiends," a derisive term similar to the label "crackhead" used by crack sellers in New York and elsewhere. Cocaine dealers said they avoided drug use, seeing it as cutting into their profits. They placed little value on being high.

Risks

Although all recognized the risks involved (being shot, robbed, or arrested), none were concerned enough to stop selling. None expressed any concern about the school zone laws, which lengthened sentences. The males said their greatest fear was the return journey from New York. They varied their routines and travel modes to conceal their activities. One cited "squealers" as another risk—evidently, some would-be dealers inform on current dealers to create their own selling opportunities.

Once they stopped selling, some said they had trouble getting used to not having as much money as when they were selling, an ironic form of dependence. Others said that day-to-day life without selling just was not as interesting. This has interesting and important implications for interventions, suggesting that more than materialism and economics is evident in drug selling (Katz, 1989).

One other risk was noted: One male who was fined was doubtful that he could pay off the fine on the earnings from his current job. If pressured by the court to pay quickly, he feared that he would have to return to selling to earn enough money to pay the fine.

Prior Records and Disposition of Arrested Drug Sellers

To better understand the law enforcement consequences that drug dealers experience, we selected a sample of adults arrested by the NPD in 1989 and obtained information from the Essex County Prosecutor on the disposition of these arrests. We also recorded New Jersey State Police criminal record information on the number of prior arrests (for drug offenses) for each member of the sample.

The population from which we drew our sample consisted of all persons included in the Narcotics Bureau database (described in Section 3) who were arrested between July 1 and November 30, 1989, for drug sales offenses. The police department sector that includes the airport was excluded. Otherwise, all Newark arrests were included in the sample population.

We wanted a sample of 200 cases, 100 from the police sectors that include the target neighborhood, Sectors 311 and 411, and 100 from outside that area. Since we found exactly 102 cases in Sectors 311 and 411, we selected all of them. We then drew a random sample of 102 cases from outside the target neighborhood sectors, so that the numbers per month would agree. We eliminated juveniles and duplicates.

Prior Records

The characteristics of those arrested for drug selling depend on both

1. The characteristics of the population actually involved in drug selling and
2. The law enforcement activities by which they are arrested.

If the police engage in a variety of undercover activities designed to arrest a wide spectrum of dealers, then the arrest population will be somewhat representative of actual dealers. However, if police arrests are concentrated on only one part of the dealer population (such as young and inexperienced street dealers), then this group will be overrepresented among arrestees. Without any information to indicate that the Newark police targeted specific types of dealers, we will presume that those arrested for selling drugs are somewhat representative of those who actually sell.

For this sample of individuals arrested for selling drugs in Newark between July and November 1989, about 80 percent had at least one prior arrest for a felony or

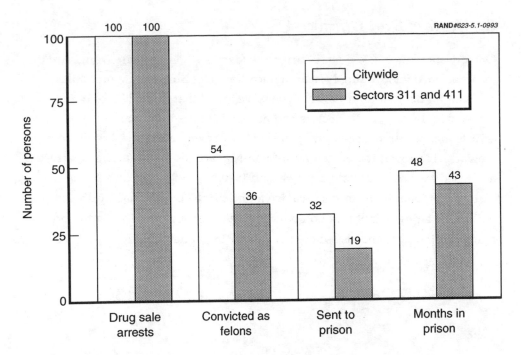

Figure 5.1—Disposition of 100 Persons Arrested in 1989 for Drug Sales Citywide
and in Newark Police Department Sectors 311 and 411

other serious offense, including drug offenses.[5] Sixty-five percent of our sample
had at least one prior adult arrest for drug offenses. Thirty-two percent had
three or more such arrests. Fifty-five percent had at least one drug arrest by the
NPD. Those arrested in the target neighborhood had fewer prior arrests than
arrestees in other parts of the city.

Arrest Outcomes

The pattern of dispositions for this sample of arrests is shown in Figure 5.1.
Citywide, about half (54 percent) were convicted of a felony charge and 32
percent receive prison terms.[6] Arrestees from the target neighborhood are less
(one-third) likely to be convicted, or sent to prison if they are. The average
prison terms received was 48 months citywide and 43 months for those arrested
in the target neighborhood.

---

[5]Prior arrests were determined by checking New Jersey State Police records, which include
adult arrests reported by law enforcement agencies throughout New Jersey. Criminal history records
for adults do not generally indicate whether or not they were ever arrested as juveniles.

[6]We do not have disposition information for the 18 percent of the sample whose cases were
referred to municipal court for prosecution.

Residence of Drug Offenders

One question often asked about drug offenders is where they are from: Are they locals or outsiders? Using Newark Police Narcotics Bureau data on adults arrested for drug sales in 1989 and 1990, we found that 84 percent of those arrested in the target area sectors had home addresses in Newark. Among arrests that occurred elsewhere in the city, 77 percent of the arrestees lived in Newark. However, the percentage of non-Newark residents among all arrestees increased in both areas between 1989 and 1990. Among those arrested in the sectors that include the target area, we found that 63 percent had addresses within the target neighborhood boundary. We were not able to identify how many of those arrested elsewhere lived in the target neighborhood.

6. Conclusions

Character of Newark's Drug Abuse Problems

By all accounts, Newark was a city with serious problems well before the current wave of drug abuse. Twenty-five years ago, racial intolerance and social injustice led to the riots of 1967, from which Newark is still recovering. During the past two decades, continued migration of middle-class residents and blue-collar jobs away from the city, and an increasingly dependent underclass, have led to declines in employment opportunities, the skills of the labor force, and the quality of life in parts of the city like the NFB target neighborhood in the Central Ward.

Among American cities, Newark ranks among the highest in rates of violent crime, indicators of substance abuse, and HIV infection. To some degree, the seriousness of these problems is probably aggravated by selective migration trends (middle-class flight and urban underclass stagnation), which have resulted in Newark having an unusually high-risk population that is disproportionately poor, minority, living in female-headed households, and in need of many remedial services. Another cause of Newark's drug problem is probably its close proximity and easy access to the drug markets of New York. Drugs are readily available and relatively inexpensive just a short train ride away.

On a per capita basis, in 1990, the number of emergency room episodes associated with either cocaine or heroin abuse in Newark exceeded that of most other major metropolitan areas. And, while the number of emergency room drug episodes reported for the greater Newark metropolitan area showed a substantial decline between 1988 and 1989, similar to that shown for the nation as a whole, the number of drug episodes experienced by Newark residents increased by 11 percent. Arrests for drug possession within the city also increased dramatically.

Cocaine continues to be the predominant street drug of choice, and it is sold most frequently in powder rather than crack cocaine form. In recent years, arrests, emergency rooms and other sources indicate that there has been a substantial increase in heroin use, by itself or in combination with cocaine. Heroin retailed in 1991 for about $15 for 25–35 milligrams. Entry into street-level dealing is relatively easy and reportedly attractive as an income generator despite the associated risks.

The extent and character of drug abuse impacts appears to vary substantially by neighborhood. The Central Ward neighborhood selected to be the initial target of NFB's efforts contains about one-quarter of the city's population but accounts for more than half of its drug-related emergency room episodes. Drug-related ER patients from this neighborhood are more likely to be 20- to 29-year-old female cocaine users, or older male heroin users, than in other parts of the city.

Potential Impacts

What are the impacts of substance abuse on Newark's other critical problems, such as health care, education, job training, employment, public safety, and housing? It probably makes them all worse, and it impedes remedial actions. People who are worrying about where they are going to get their next high are usually not very good at focusing on other, longer-term problems. Citizens who are afraid to answer their doors or venture out in their neighborhoods are difficult to get organized into an effective political or social force.

Rather than just being causally linked, problems like substance abuse, homelessness, and school failure may also be common symptoms of a larger underlying phenomenon—such as a declining economic base and fewer job opportunities for low-skilled workers. In that case, dealing with only the symptoms is not going to have much impact on long-term trends. What would also be needed is a policy to reverse the declining fortunes of the city or one for dispersing its residents to areas where the economy is growing. To some degree, both of these policy directions are being pursued, as shown by the city's loss of 16 percent of its population during the past decade and by its vigorous pursuit of new employers in the educational and service sectors.

Although there are no data specific to Newark, we have no reason to believe that recent trends there differ significantly from observed nationwide trends toward declining prevalence rates, increased perceptions of the harms associated with drug use, and fewer new users. These findings pertain to the general population as measured through student and household surveys. Among students surveyed in New Jersey, those in urban areas and those in low-income categories report the same declining drug use as those in suburban and more affluent communities. If the same is true and could be documented specifically for Newark students, it would be encouraging news but hardly suggestive that an end to Newark's drug problems is in sight.

Unlike trends in drug use among the general population, the problems associated with chronic drug abuse—crime; violence and disruption of neighborhoods where drug dealing is prominent; and serious health effects, including HIV infection, increased mortality rates, and ever-increasing demands for public resources to support treatment services—have not declined in Newark or in most other major urban areas. Of course, we would expect the consequences of drug abuse to linger even after declines in the rate of use take place. But if declines in use are only occurring among the relatively low-risk portion of the population (such as students and householders), while high-risk populations (dropouts, chronic truants, the homeless, incarcerated offenders, etc.) continue to use at high rates,[1] drugs will continue to produce high rates of the problems associated with their chronic use. This situation will be greatly exacerbated if the high-risk populations themselves increase in number or retain their members over longer periods of time.

Prevention and Risks for Youth

Our first presumption, given the high rate of substance abuse exhibited by adults, was that all Newark youth had to be considered at risk for substance abuse and treated accordingly. We are now no longer sure that this is the case. The New Jersey Department of Law and Public Safety Survey of New Jersey high school students, and other surveys of teenage youth, provide no evidence to suggest that youth who live in cities like Newark are any more at risk of substance abuse than those who live in other locations. If, in fact, prevalence rates increase dramatically among Newark youth after they leave high school, additional surveys are needed to establish this fact, and new prevention programs need to be developed that target this group, since most prevention efforts are directed at a considerably younger age group.

At present, there is not a wide range of opportunities for young men 14 to 18 years of age in Newark to earn income or prove their mettle. Becoming a drug seller does both. Most of the young male sellers we talked with were initially sponsored by an older dealer (possibly a relative, acquaintance, or someone the youth sought out), who fronted them a small amount of drugs. In addition to netting several hundred dollars every full day they work, young sellers like being involved in the process of packaging and selling drugs and the respect that their involvement brings them.

The way the screening by older dealers seems to work, the young males who are selected to participate and advance in the trade are those who are able to build

---

[1]Surveys of hidden chronic-use groups, such as arrestees, have indicated extremely high drug-use rates compared to the general population.

up a clientele and demonstrate they are trustworthy in handling drugs and cash. These are just the youth who also would be most likely to do well in legitimate activities if they were given the opportunity or if there were some immediate payoff. Therefore, it would seem that the drug trade might attract some of the more ambitious and talented youth in the community.

Young men who become involved in the drug trade face considerable risks: being shot by other dealers, an unhappy customer, or the stickup boys; getting arrested and having to do time in a correctional program; acquiring a criminal record and associates; or getting gradually sucked into using drugs as one of the constant temptations of the trade. All of these risks detract from the likelihood of long-term success for Newark's youth.

What can law enforcement do about this situation, especially when there appear to be a large number of backup sellers waiting for their chances to move in whenever someone else is arrested? The only option for increasing the deterrent effects of current enforcement options is to increase the likelihood of arrest, by increasing the frequency of undercover buys, or by increasing the severity of sanctions. However, currently, most adults arrested for drug sales have long prior records, and those convicted and incarcerated (about one-third of arrestees) receive an average sentence of four years and end up serving around 18 months. One other approach that might be tried is education aimed at decreasing the respect that young dealers claim they enjoy and increasing the respect afforded those who succeed at more legitimate pursuits (such as sports or participation in an urban service corps) that can provide an alternative way for young men to earn the esteem of their peers.

Less is known about the incentives of young women to become involved in drug dealing. However, arrest figures suggest that they become involved later than males, which may imply different motivations and therefore will require different interventions to prevent and deter. Law enforcement policies may have much to do with the apparent differences between males and females. Teenage boys may be more subject to arrest than teenage girls for the same behavior. Having been arrested starting at an earlier age, adult males who continue in drug dealing may be incarcerated in their late twenties and thirties for longer periods than women. It might be that females are recruited to drug dealing by the men they associate with in their early twenties. There may also be different economic incentives for males and females.

Treatment

Unfortunately, substance abuse is not a problem that is quickly cured with even the best forms of treatment. Many substance-abusing individuals will require sustained and continued involvement in programs for many years to come. This is probably especially true in cluster areas like the NFB Central Ward target neighborhood, where drug use indicators suggest there are large concentrations of older heroin users.

In theory, the citizens of Newark have access to the full range of treatment programs, from detoxification and long-term residential treatment through intensive day care, methadone maintenance, drug-free outpatient, and aftercare. However, in practice, many segments of the population appear to be underserved, particularly women with children, the elderly, and indigents in need of residential treatment or aftercare. The availability of services for these particular groups is limited by restrictions on the type of clients handled or services provided by many existing programs, or the special needs of their members (like child care) that are not being met by existing programs.

Although the existence of these service gaps is recognized by many in the drug treatment community, the magnitude of the gaps is difficult to determine. Better information on the unmet treatment needs of drug users in Newark can only be obtained from periodic household surveys or surveys and/or drug testing of specific high-risk groups (such as offenders or school dropouts), or systematic tracking and case management of all those seeking to enter treatment. The latter approach has the added advantage of providing a means of identifying and targeting specific high-priority individuals at a point when they appear most willing to begin the recovery process.

Closing Reflections

More than a year has now passed since a draft of this report was first presented to members of the NFB project. Since that time, the Newark project has been awarded a substantial grant from the Robert Wood Johnson Foundation to implement the programs and procedural reforms that were developed in response to this study. During the past year, we have conducted studies involving many of the same issues that we dealt with in this report—at the local, state, and national levels.

Nothing that we have learned in the course of these studies would cause us to change any of the basic conclusions we reached concerning the nature of Newark's drug problems, or its options for responding to them. Most programs that were described as promising several years ago are still just that—promising, but untested possibilities. To our knowledge, no one has solved the problem of how to keep ambitious young inner-city males from participating in the drug trade. Granted, the returns for most participants are relatively modest; the profits still probably look attractive compared to those available in inner-city areas through legitimate opportunities (Reuter et al., 1990). In fact, participation in drug dealing was one of the principal risk factors that accounted for a high rate of recidivism among young men returning from court-ordered placements to the city of Pittsburgh (Greenwood and Deschenes, 1993).

To our knowledge, no one has solved the problem of how to improve the match between clients and programs as a way of making treatment more effective and reducing the extremely high attrition rates. In fact, most of the cities that have attempted to develop some form of centralized intake and case-management systems, as part of the Center for Substance Abuse Treatment's Target Cities Program have experienced considerable problems and delays in implementing those functions.

The good news is that there appear to be more programs devoted to the special needs of women, particularly those with children. Another bright spot is the development of treatment alternatives to prison or jail for drug-involved offenders in the criminal justice system. Specialized drug courts in Miami, Oakland, and Phoenix, and a number of Treatment Alternatives to Street Crime programs throughout the country, have demonstrated that proper incentives and close supervision by the court can be used to encourage criminal justice clients to comply with the requirements of fairly rigorous outpatient treatment programs (Tauber, 1993; United States General Accounting Office, 1993). An additional factor that will affect Newark's ability to deal with its drug problem but did not loom as large during the course of our study is the precarious condition of most state and local budgets. Many jurisdictions have been cutting into essential services as they are forced to reduce their budgets by 10 to 20 percent, for several years in a row. The amount of funding available for the prevention or treatment of drug problems is not likely to rise under the current circumstances. These tightened fiscal conditions only increase the pressure on local health, law enforcement, and political leaders to devise creative prevention and treatment strategies that draw upon resources already available within the community, rather than waiting for outside help. Careful delineation and scrutiny of the risk factors that apply to specific neighborhoods or community groups and sensible adaptation, refinement, and testing of programmatic concepts that have shown promise in other sites are the strategies that are likely to distinguish the more successful local efforts (Hawkins and Catalano, 1992). Now, more than ever, the availability and quality of drug prevention and treatment services will depend on the persistence and wisdom of local leaders and program administrators in how they target those efforts.

Appendix
A. Partial List of Collateral Service Providers

American Rescue Mission
84 Magazine St.
Newark, NJ 07105
George Gossett, Director
201-589-5772

Essex County Jail Programs
60 Nelson Place
Newark, NJ 07103
Paul DeBellis, Coordinator
201-621-5154

Goodwill Home Mission
79 University Avenue
Newark, NJ 07102
David Scott, Director
201-621-9560

National Community Health
741 Broadway
Newark, NJ 07104
Dr. Robert Russell, Director
201-483-1300

National Council on Alcoholism
(N.C.A.)
North Jersey Area, Inc.—
Newark Branch
303-9 Washington Street
Newark, NJ 07102
Joyce Love, Director
201-242-7406

Protestant Community Centers, Inc.
256 N. 7th Street
Newark, NJ 07107
Tony L. Peele, Executive Director
201-481-2855

United Labor Agency of Essex—
West Hudson, Inc.
10 Park Place
Newark, NJ 07102
Robert Cawley, Executive Director
201-623-7878

Work Oriented Rehabilitation
Institute
15 Roseville Ave.
Newark, NJ 07107
Lewis Garley, Executive Director
201-733-4759

B. Source List for Newark Substance Abuse Treatment Providers

1. Fighting Back Staff

2. Fighting Back Project Substance Abuse Committee List

3. Newark Health Behavior Project Resource Manual, 1990

4. New Jersey Dept. of Health Division of Alcoholism and Drug Abuse *Directory of Drug Abuse Treatment and Rehabilitation Facilities*, 1989

5. Essex County Division of Alcoholism and Drug Abuse, 1991 Grantees Address List

6. Newark Telephone Directory

7. *Drug, Alcohol, and Other Addictions: A Directory of Treatment Centers and Prevention Programs Nationwide*, The Oryx Press, 1989

8. *National Directory of Drug Abuse and Alcoholism Treatment and Prevention Programs*, National Institute on Drug Abuse, 1989

9. *AHA Hospital Statistics—A Comprehensive Summary of U.S. Hospitals 1990–91*, The American Hospital Association

10. *1989 National Treatment Directory for Alcoholism, Drug Abuse, and Other Addiction Problems*, The U.S. Journal of Drug and Alcohol Dependence, Inc., 1988

C. Substance Abuse Treatment Providers

Catholic Community Services
(C.C.S.)
17 Mulberry Street
Newark, NJ 07102

Choices, Inc.
169 Roseville Avenue
Newark, NJ 07107

Community United for Rehab of
the Addicted (CURA), Inc.
Administration Office
35 Lincoln Park
Newark, NJ 07102

East Orange General Hospital
Addiction Services
300 Central Ave.
East Orange, NJ 07019

Essex Substance Abuse Treatment
Center, Inc.
164 Blanchard Street
Newark, NJ 07105

Integrity Inc.
Administrative Office
103 Lincoln Park
P.O. Box 1806
Newark, NJ 07102

La Casa De Don Pedro
Central Administration
75 Park Ave.
Newark, NJ 07104

Multiphasic Drug Treatment
Program*
Central Intake & Detox Unit
15 Roseville Ave.
Newark, NJ 07107

Newark Renaissance House, Inc.
P.O. Box 7057
Newark, NJ 07107

New Well Rehabilitation Center*
15 Roseville Avenue
Newark, NJ 07107

St. Michael's Hospital
268 Martin Luther King Blvd.
Newark, NJ 07102

Spectrum Health Care
461 Frelinghuysen Avenue
Newark, NJ 07114

Straight & Narrow, Inc.
508 Straight St.
Paterson, NJ 07501

Turning Point, Inc.
Box 111
Verona, NJ 07044

United Community Corporation
(U.C.C.)
31 Fulton St.
Newark, NJ 07102

*Deleted from survey because
programs no longer in operation.

University of Medicine
& Dentistry–New Jersey
Alcoholism Treatment Center
ADMC Rm 1412
30 Bergen Street
Newark, NJ 07107-3000

Veterans Administration Medical
Center
East Orange, NJ 07019

Volunteers of America
155 Washington St., Room 201
Newark, NJ 07102

D. Newark Substance Abuse Prevention Programs Partial List

AD House
13 Clinton Place
Newark, NJ 07108

Black Churchmen's Task Force
Newark, NJ

Boys' and Girls' Clubs of Newark
35 James Street
Newark, NJ 07102

The Bridge, Inc.
14 Park Avenue
Caldwell, NJ 07006

Catholic Community Services
17 Mulberry Street
Newark, NJ 07102

Community Mental Health Services
570 Belleville Avenue
Belleville, NJ 07109

Community United for Rehab of
the Addicted (CURA), Inc.
35 Lincoln Park
Newark, NJ 07102

Essex County College
303 University Avenue
Newark, NJ 07102

Essex County Prosecutor's
Community Task Force
60 Nelson Place
Newark, NJ 07103

Integrity House, Inc.
103 Lincoln Park
P. O. Box 1806
Newark, NJ 07102

International Youth Organization
703 South 12th Street
Newark, NJ 07102

La Casa De Don Pedro
Central Administration
75 Park Avenue
Newark, NJ 07104

Main St. Counseling Center
345 Main Street
West Orange, NJ 07052

National Black Alcoholism
Council, Inc.
New Jersey Chapter
41 Rector Street
Newark, NJ 07101

National Council on Alcoholism
(N.C.A.)
North Jersey Area, Inc.—
Newark Branch
303-9 Washington Street
Newark, NJ 07102

Newark Beth Israel
Medical Center /CMHC
Early Screening & Intervention
Program
201 Lyons Avenue
Newark, NJ 07112

Newark Board of Education
2 Cedar Street
Newark, NJ 07102

Newark Renaissance House, Inc.
P. O. Box 7057
Newark, NJ 07107

New Jersey EAS Northern Office
744 Broad Street
Newark, NJ 07102

North Essex Development & Action
Council, Inc. (N.E.D.A.C.)
104 Bloomfield Avenue
Montclair, NJ 07042

Prevention of Child Abuse—
NJ Chapter
17 Academy St., Suite 709
Newark, NJ 07102

Special Audiences
75 Ferry Street
Newark, NJ 07105

Turning Point, Inc.—
Newark Branch YMWCA
6000 Broad Street, Rooms 108/109
Newark, NJ 07102

United Community Corporation
(U.C.C.)
31 Fulton Street
Newark, NJ 07102

United Labor Agency of
Essex–West Hudson, Inc.
10 Park Place
Newark, NJ 07102

UMDNJ-Teen Powerhouse
c/o Essex County Vocational School
91 West Market St.
Newark, NJ 07102

UMDNJ-Dept. of Pediatrics
185 So. Orange Avenue
Newark, NJ 07103

West Orange Family Youth Service
and Child Guidance Center of the
Oranges, Milburn, Maplewood
4 Charles Street
West Orange, NJ 07052

E. AIDS Among Newark City Residents
(as of April 30, 1991)

AIDS Among Newark City Residents (as of April 30, 1991)

1. Disease Category

	Adult/Adolescent				Pediatric				Total			
	Cases	(%)	Deaths	(%)	Cases	(%)	Deaths	(%)	Cases	(%)	Deaths	(%)
Pneumocystis carinii pneumonia (PCP)	1,087	(51)	691	(64)	22	(25)	14	(64)	1,109	(50)	705	(64)
Other disease w/o PCP	1,024	(48)	638	(62)	67	(75)	32	(48)	1,091	(49)	670	(61)
Kaposi's sarcoma alone	33	(2)	24	(73)	0	(0)	0	(0)	33	(1)	24	(73)
No diseases listed	0	(0)	0	(0)	0	(0)	0	(0)	0	(0)	0	(0)
Total	2,144	(100)	1,353	(63)	89	(100)	46	(52)	2,233	(100)	1,399	(63)

2. Age

	Cases	(%)
Under 5	73	(3)
5–12	16	(1)
13–19	9	(0)
20–29	351	(16)
30–39	1,150	(52)
40–49	456	(20)
Over 49	178	(8)
Total	2,233	(100)

3. Race/Ethnicity

	Adult/Adolescent		Pediatric		Total	
	Cases	(%)	Cases	(%)	Cases	(%)
White, not hispanic	99	(5)	3	(3)	102	(5)
Black, not hispanic	1,824	(85)	71	(80)	1,895	(85)
Hispanic	218	(10)	15	(17)	233	(10)
Other/unknown	3	(0)	0	(0)	3	(0)
Total	2,144	(100)	89	(100)	2,233	(100)

4. Patient Groups

Adult/Adolescent

	Males	(%)	Females	(%)	Total
Homosexual or bisexual men	290	(19)	0	(0)	290
IVDU	1,033	(68)	442	(71)	1,475
Homosexual/bisexual IVDU	83	(5)	0	(0)	83
Hemophiliac	7	(0)	0	(0)	7
Heterosexual contact	65	(4)	148	(24)	213
Born in NIR country	22	(1)	6	(1)	28
Transfusion with blood/products	6	(0)	15	(2)	21
None of the above/other	16	(1)	11	(2)	27
Total	1,522	(100)	622	(100)	2,144

Pediatric

	Males	(%)	Females	(%)	Total
Hemophiliac/transfusion related	1	(2)	0	(0)	1
Parent at risk/has AIDS/HIV	45	(98)	43	(100)	88
None of the above/other	0	(0)	0	(0)	0
Total	46	(100)	43	(100)	89

SOURCE: New Jersey Department of Health, AIDS Data Analysis Unit, April 30, 1991.

References

1989 National Treatment Directory for Alcoholism, Drug Abuse, and Other Addiction Problems, The U.S. Journal of Drug and Alcohol Dependence, Inc., 1989.

AHA Hospital Statistics—A Comprehensive Summary of U.S. Hospitals 1990–91, The American Hospital Association.

American Housing Survey for the Northern NJ Metropolitan Area in 1987, Bureau of the Census, Current Housing Reports H-170-87-10, U.S. Department of Commerce, June 1990.

Bartlett, Jacqueline A., Steven J. Schleifer, Robert L. Johnson, and Steven E. Keller, "Depression in Inner City Adolescents Attending an Adolescent Medicine Clinic," *Journal of Adolescent Health*, Vol. 12, 1991, pp. 316–318.

Board of Education, *Annual Report of Dropouts*, Newark, New Jersey Board of Education, 1988.

Board of Education, *Annual Report of Dropouts*, Newark, New Jersey Board of Education, 1989.

Board of Education, *Annual Report of Dropouts*, Newark, New Jersey Board of Education, 1990.

Botvin, Gilbert J., "Substance Abuse Prevention: Theory, Practice, and Effectiveness," in Michael Tonry and James Q. Wilson, *Drugs and Crime*, University of Chicago Press, 1990.

Bourgois, P., "In Search of Horatio Alger: Culture and Ideology in the Crack Economy," *Contemporary Drug Problems*, Vol. 16, No. 4, 1989, pp. 619–650.

Bureau of the Census, *Characteristics of Households and Families*, 1980, U.S. Department of Commerce.

Chavis, D. M., R. Kopacsi, and A. J. Lazarus, *Community Problem Study: Report on Public Opinion to the United Way of Essex/West Hudson*, Center for Community Education, School of Social Work, Rutgers University, May 1989.

Coleman, Claude, "Memorandum to All Commands," November 26, 1990.

Cunningham, John T., *Newark*, The New Jersey Historical Society, Newark, New Jersey, 1988.

Department of Health, Division of Alcoholism and Drug Abuse, Office of Data Analysis and Epidemiology, *Statistical Perspectives on Alcoholism Treatment in New Jersey 1988*, July 1990.

Department of Health, Division of Alcoholism and Drug Abuse Office of Data Analysis and Epidemiology, *Statistical Perspectives on Drug Abuse Treatment in New Jersey 1989*, September, 1990.

Dickens, Bernard, Testimony Before Committee on Education and Labor, Subcommittee on Select Education Hearing, Abandoned Infants Assistance Act, May 10, 1991.

Drug, Alcohol, and Other Addictions: A Directory of Treatment Centers and Prevention Programs Nationwide, The Oryx Press, 1989.

Ellickson, Phyllis L., and Robert M. Bell, *Prospects for Preventing Drug Use Among Young Adolescents*, Santa Monica, Calif.: RAND, R-3896-CHF, 1990.

Elliott, Delbert S., David Huizinga, and Scott Menard, *Multiple Problem Youth: Delinquency, Substance Use, and Mental Health Problems*, Springer-Verlag, New York, 1989.

Fagan, Jeffrey,"Drug Selling and Licit Income in Distressed Neighborhoods: The Economic Lives of Street-level Drug Users and Dealers," presented at the Conference of Drugs, Crime and Social Distress, Urban Opportunity Program of the Urban Institute, Philadelphia, April, 1991.

Federal Bureau of Investigation, *Uniform Crime Report (UCR)*, U.S. Department of Justice, 1989.

Fisher, Wayne S., *Drug and Alcohol Use Among New Jersey High School Students*, New Jersey Department of Law and Public Safety, 1990.

Freeman, R.B., "Crime and the Economic Status of Disadvantaged Young Men," presented at the Conference on Labor Markets and Urban Mobility, The Urban Institute, Washington, D.C., 1991.

French, John F., "Patterns of Drug Use in Newark," in *Epidemiologic Trends in Drug Abuse, Community Epidemiology Work Group* (CEWG), *Proceedings June, 1990*, U.S. Department of Health and Human Services, 1990.

French, John F., "Patterns of Drug Use in Newark," in *Epidemiologic Trends in Drug Abuse, Community Epidemiology Work Group* (CEWG), *Proceedings December, 1990*, U.S. Department of Health and Human Services, 1991a.

French, John F., "Patterns of Drug Use in Newark," in *Epidemiologic Trends in Drug Abuse, Community Epidemiology Work Group* (CEWG), *Proceedings June, 1991*, U.S. Department of Health and Human Services, 1991b.

Greenwood, Peter W., and Elizabeth Piper Deschenes, *The Effects of Intensive Aftercare on the Post-Release Behavior of Chronic Juvenile Offenders*, RAND, Santa Monica, Calif., MR-220-SKF, forthcoming.

Greenwood, Peter W., "Substance Abuse Problems Among High-Risk Youth and Potential Interventions," *Crime & Delinquency*, Vol. 38, No. 4, 1992.

Hawkins, J. David, Richard F. Catalano, Jr., and Associates, *Communities That Care: Action for Drug Abuse Prevention*, Jossey-Bass, San Francisco, Calif., 1992.

Johnson, Bruce D., Terry Williams, Kojo A. Dei, and Harry Sanabria, "Drug Abuse in the Inner City: Impact on Hard-drug Users and the Community," in Michael Tonry and James Q. Wilson, *Drugs and Crime*, The University of Chicago Series on Crime and Justice, Vol. 13, 1990.

Katz, Jack, *The Seductions of Crime*, Basic Books, New York, 1989.

Miller, Rena, "As Cocaine Comes off a High, Heroin May be Filling Void," *The Los Angeles Times*, June 19, 1991.

National Center for Health Statistics, *Vital Statistics of the United States*, Public Health Service, Washington, D.C.: U.S. Government Printing Office, 1990.

National Institute on Drug Abuse, *National Directory of Drug Abuse and Alcoholism Treatment and Prevention Programs*, U.S. Department of Health and Human Services, 1989.

New Jersey Department of Health, Division of Alcoholism and Drug Abuse, *Directory of Drug Abuse Treatment and Rehabilitation Facilities*, 1989.

New Jersey Statutes, 18A:35-4.

Newark Police Department, *Annual Statistical Report 1989*, Newark, New Jersey, 1990.

Newark Police Department, *Annual Statistical Report 1990*, Newark, New Jersey, 1990.

Reiss, Albert J., Jr., and Jeffrey A. Roth (eds.), *Understanding and Preventing Violence*, National Academy of Science, Washington, D.C., National Academy Press, 1993.

Reuter, Peter, MacCoun, Robert, Murphy, Patrick, with Allan Abrahamse, Barbara Simon, *Money from Crime: A Study of the Economics of Drug Dealing in Washington*, Santa Monica, Calif.: RAND, R-3894-RF, 1990.

Sheppard, David, and A. Pate, *Operation Homestead in Newark*, prepared for the Attorney General of the State of New Jersey, Police Foundation, Washington, D.C., 1991.

Skogan, Wesley G., *Disorder and Decline: Crime and the Spiral of Decay in American Neighborhoods*, University of California Press, Los Angeles, Calif., 1990.

Tauber, Jeffrey S., *The Importance of Immediate Intervention in a Comprehensive Court-Ordered Drug Rehabilitation Program*, A Preliminary Evaluation of the F.I.R.S.T. Diversion Project (Fast, Intensive, Report, Supervision and Treatment), Drug Diversion Program of the Oakland-Piedmont-Emeryville Municipal Court and the Alameda (Calif.) County Probation Dept., presented at the Presidential Commission on Model State Drug Laws, March 10, 1993.

Tierney, John, "In Newark, A Spiral of Drugs and AIDS," *The New York Times*, December 19, 1991.

U.S. Department of Commerce, *Statistical Abstract of the United States*, 1990.

104

U.S. General Accounting Office, "Drug Control: Treatment Alternatives Program for Drug Offenders Needs Stronger Emphasis," U.S. Government Printing Office, Washington, D.C., 1993.

Viscusi, W. Kip, "Market Incentives for Criminal Behavior," in Richard Freeman and Harry Holzer (eds.), *The Youth Employment Crisis*, University of Chicago Press, 1986.